START HERE NOW

START

an open-hearted guide

HERE

to the path and practice

NOW

of meditation

Susan Piver

SHAMBHALA • Boston & London • 2015

Shambhala Publications, Inc.
Horticultural Hall
300 Massachusetts Avenue
Boston, Massachusetts 02115
www.shambhala.com

9 8 7 6 5 4 3 2 1

FIRST EDITION
Printed in the United States of America

♾This edition is printed on acid-free paper that meets the
American National Standards Institute z39.48 Standard.
♻Shambhala Publications makes every effort to print on recycled paper.
For more information please visit www.shambhala.com.
Distributed in the United States by Penguin Random House LLC
and in Canada by Random House of Canada Ltd

Designed by K. E. White

LIBRARY OF CONGRESS CATALOGING-IN-PUBLICATION DATA
Piver, Susan.
Start here now: an open-hearted guide to the path and
practice of meditation / Susan Piver.
pages   cm
ISBN 978-1-61180-267-2 (paperback)
1. Meditation—Buddhism. I. Title.
BQ5612.P59 2015
294.3'4435—dc23
2014047499

To my esteemed meditation students and members of the Open Heart Project for inspiring me with their practice.

To my teacher, Sakyong Mipham Rinpoche, for teaching me everything I know.

To his father, Chögyam Trungpa Rinpoche, for teaching me everything I don't know.

To my treasured spiritual friend and meditation instructor who shall remain nameless because he prefers it that way for some reason, for ushering me onto the path with so much love and precision.

And in memory of my beloved father, Julius Piver, for teaching me how to finish the job.

My gratitude to each is the beacon that lights my way.

CONTENTS

	Introduction	1
1.	Benefits	7
2.	What Meditation Is	14
3.	What Meditation Is Not	24
4.	Common Misconceptions	25
5.	Kinds of Meditation	31
6.	Three Yanas	41
7.	How to Choose	48
8.	Our Practice: Shamatha	52
9.	How to Meditate	59
10.	Tips for Establishing Your Practice	65
11.	On Posture	70
12.	Setting Up Your Space	78
13.	Keeping It Sacred	81
14.	Obstacles and Antidotes	86
15.	Meditation and Depression	91

16. Meditation and Creativity   95
17. Meditation and Compassion   99
18. Meditation and Love   104
19. Aspire: The Seven-Day Meditation
    Challenge   112
20. To Deepen: A Weekend Meditation
    Retreat at Home   118
    Epilogue: Personal Story   134
    Appendix A: FAQs   144
    Appendix B: Important Figures   167
    Appendix C: Resources   175
    Acknowledgments   179
    About the Author   181

START HERE NOW

INTRODUCTION

If you want to meditate but have no idea where to begin, this book will help you.

If you used to meditate and are looking for a way to reenter your practice, this book will help you.

If you know you want to try meditation but are reluctant for any reason to go to a meditation center, this book will help you to try it without risk or nervousness.

In all cases, we are going to Start Here. Now!

Welcome to *Start Here Now: An Open-Hearted Guide to the Path and Practice of Meditation*. This book contains everything you need to know to start a meditation practice and, even more important, to *continue* one. It defines what meditation is (and what it is not), offers tips for making the practice a part of your life, dispels the most common misconceptions, describes the obstacles we all face and how to navigate them, and addresses the most frequently asked questions. I give you a concise overview of the various popular styles of Buddhist meditation and offer suggestions should you want to explore them further. Most important, this book contains specific, concrete, actionable steps for beginning your own meditation practice in a stress-free, dogma-free, jargon-free way.

Meditation is more than a practice; it is a way of being in the world. It is a path. In this book, I have also tried to describe some of the ways your practice carries over into your off-the-cushion life to increase self-confidence, improve relationships, enhance creativity, and create a foundation for working with strong emotion.

Though this book can stand alone as a guide, there are two self-paced programs that can go along with it. The first, a seven-day meditation challenge (in chapter 19), lays out a detailed plan for slowly but surely—and simply—introducing the practice to your life, which I'm sure is already quite busy and full. Still, it is totally possible to make time for meditation and this program shows you how. I've created seven guided meditation videos to support and guide you each day of this challenge and you can access them anytime at my website, www.susanpiver.com/shn-resources. The second is a complete plan for creating a weekend meditation retreat at home.

Okay, let's face it. Starting a meditation practice is not that difficult. I've started mine countless times! What is difficult is *sustaining* the practice. As founder of the Open Heart Project, an online community of more than twelve thousand meditators all over the world who have been receiving weekly meditation instruction from me for three years, I've learned a lot about what helps you to keep going. I've put all of that information into this book and, if you are interested, my website also includes a self-guided program with different lessons which you may learn more about at www.susanpiver.com/shn-resources.

If you are serious about making meditation practice an ongoing part of your life, this book is for you. I will be with you each step of the way.

I have had the extraordinary good fortune to be trained by brilliant, compassionate, realized teachers. It is my delight to share with you what I've learned over nearly two decades of Buddhist study and practice. Though I have done my best to understand what I have been taught and bring it into my experience so that I can share it with you, I am not being humble when I say that my mind may not be big enough to grasp these profound teachings. Therefore, I may have made mistakes. If so, this is a reflection of my own lack of understanding, not of any flaw in their teachings.

. . .

I've been practicing Buddhist meditation since 1993 and took formal vows as a Buddhist in 1995. In 2004, I completed a deeper course of study in a seminary in my lineage (Shambhala Buddhism, a Tibetan school). It was only then that I was eligible to take training as a meditation instructor, which I did in 2005.

Since that time, I have taught meditation to people all over the world. I have led retreats on meditation and creativity, meditation and relationships, meditation and mindful communication, meditation and . . . meditation. I've authored eight books that have been translated into thirteen languages. I have written and spoken about meditation and its impact on everyday life for close to a decade now.

In 2011, I started what has turned into the largest nondenominational online mindfulness community in the world, the Open Heart Project. As of this writing, there are over twelve thousand members who sit down to meditate with me every day. I lead online retreats for them, teach classes for them virtually, and create and email new meditation instructional videos to this growing group of wonderful, smart, independent-minded seekers in more than forty countries. Thus I have given meditation instruction countless times! I've counseled many people on how to work with the difficulties of establishing the practice as a part of everyday life. I've come to know the most frequently asked questions and the most commonly encountered obstacles. Throughout, I've had the honor of hearing many, many stories about the positive impact of meditation practice on difficult emotions, depressions, relationship problems, physical injuries and illnesses, traumas, boredom, frustration, and confusion. I've developed a great appreciation for what it takes to establish a consistent meditation practice, and I want to share with you what I've learned so that you too can make this exceedingly simple and profound practice a part of your life.

We live in a time where the benefits of mindfulness meditation have been demonstrated beyond doubt. It is likely that somewhere, someone—whether a doctor, friend, colleague, or author—has said to you, dear reader: "You should learn to meditate."

That time has come!

ONE

• • •

benefits

A comprehensive list of all the benefits of meditation would be very long indeed. My friend and fellow meditation teacher Jonathan Foust has said that if it were a medication, meditation would be heralded as the miracle drug of the century! Some of the benefits that have been demonstrated recently through modern scientific inquiry include the following:

It relieves stress (by lowering the stress hormone, cortisol).

It improves focus and memory (by raising the level of gamma waves).

It prevents relapse into depression by 50 percent

(according to studies by Jon Kabat-Zinn, MD, and Zindel Segal, PhD).

It boosts immunity (in one study, meditators demonstrated higher levels of antibodies than nonmeditators in reaction to a vaccination).

It actually makes you demonstrably happier (by reducing activation in the amygdala and increasing it in the prefrontal cortex).

The health benefits don't stop there. In addition, it has been demonstrated that meditation can help with the following:

lowering blood pressure

decreasing symptoms in illnesses with a stress-related component (ulcers, for example)

decreasing serum cholesterol levels

reducing muscular tension

reducing oxygen and energy consumption

improving sleep

In short, it has been scientifically proven that meditation is awesome.

Other sorts of benefits have been recounted in reports from countless meditators over thousands of years. To this amazing list, add that for millennia, saints, yogis, and gurus have been urging meditation as a way to become more peaceful, kind, and wise. It is offered as the foundation for a life of sanity and joy. It is counseled as a way to increase loving kindness and compassion for all. It is even taught as a path to enlightenment and lasting bliss.

From relieving stress to complete liberation from suffering: this is one amazing technique.

To this, I will add the benefits that I have discovered for myself and from my students. Whether they are from Manhattan or Mumbai, Manila or Madrid, I have heard the following recounted time and again.

Meditation gives you the courage to be who you are.

Somehow, the act of sitting down with yourself with the willingness to simply *be* with yourself as you are, whether you show up in your most brilliant or puniest form, relaxes the inner critic or whatever stands behind our oppressive self-criticism and incessant efforts to improve ourselves. Meditation says, "I don't care if you are the most excellent person of all time or the most absurd—I love you. Right now." This is the love that most of us have never received. Surprisingly, it doesn't look like affection or approval. It looks like companionship. If you've ever wished for a friend who would love you as you are, appreciate your genius, and make space for your foibles, welcome you when you're funny and shiny *and* when you're a complete mess—

well, I can introduce you to this person. Rather, your meditation practice can. He or she has been there the whole time. You are the one you've been waiting for, as they say.

As you surf your inner environment and just hang out with yourself, you practice self-acceptance. It has nothing to do with finally becoming the person you have always wanted to be (whoever that is), but instead it is about constantly affirming your allegiance to . . . yourself. From this, courage naturally arises. You see that your thoughts are always trying to seduce you in one way or another—to get mad about something, crave something, avoid something; to become busier, less busy, nicer, sterner, taller, shorter, and so on. In an untrained state, we always go along for the ride. But when you train your mind through the practice of meditation, you see that no matter how many thoughts arise that tell you to become furious or desirous or sleepy or frenzied, they all, eventually, pass. Always.

With each moment that you wait, you soften—first toward yourself and then toward others, which leads to the second benefit that I always hear about.

Meditation makes you like your fellow humans more.

The practice of meditation has one particularly unexpected side effect. I did not anticipate this one and, as far as I can tell from my fellow practitioners and meditation students, they did not either.

As it chips away at your concepts, stories, and judgments, meditation opens your heart.

Why are these two things related? How is it that sitting on the ground "doing nothing" softens your heart?

Because when you give up your story about yourself and about life, you are left with things as they are.

When you don't take refuge in stories, you forgo the protection of conventional wisdom, unexamined projections, and biases of all kinds. You are basically raw and there is nowhere to hide.

When you're open, unguarded, and inquisitive, you feel everything. You see that not only are you incredibly vulnerable, so is everyone else. In becoming gentler toward yourself, you become gentler toward others. All of this seems to happen without your willing it to.

When it does, your fellow humans cease to be devices in your plans for happiness and instead become actual individuals with joys and sorrows, both of which you can feel. You see that everyone, *everyone*, is as unprotected as you are and is pretending that they are not. So your heart goes out to them, even the ones you think are jerks. You can no longer treat anyone as less than yourself. Rather than "us and them," you see that the world is just us.

Meditation helps you see the magic of this world.

When you have a sense of gentleness toward yourself and others, something quite extraordinary happens. You relax. Whether things go well or poorly on any particular day you can deal with it because you know how to remain soft and open. This soft openness is the same thing as waking up to the present moment. You are right here, open to your life and this world.

In the present moment, the natural wisdom, beauty, and peace of your own mind and this world are always apparent. Profound wisdom in the form of awareness cuts through your concepts again and again. The simple act of meditation, of placing awareness on breath and, when it strays, bringing it back, is exactly, precisely, utterly this act of wisdom.

If you've meditated before, you have seen this. You know that at some point during meditation your mind wanders and then, somehow, something in there says, "Hey, you're thinking—you're supposed to be paying attention to your breath." You're wandering around in a sea of hope, fear, boredom, excitement, and so on, when, out of nowhere, awareness cuts in to remind you of what you are supposed to be doing.

Where does that come from?

Well, unfortunately I do not know, but I do know that it is the same place that creative inspiration comes from, and insight, and love. As your practice progresses, these are your reward. So don't be afraid of the softness, openness, and groundlessness that can accompany the giving up of concepts. This groundlessness can feel quite odd at first. But in the words of the Tibetan meditation master Chögyam Trungpa, "The bad news is you're falling through the air, nothing to hang on to, no parachute. The good news is there's no ground."

Personally, I could tell you that meditation has made me happier and better able to deal with stress. I could tell you that it has made me more patient and kind. I could tell you that since becoming a meditator, I have learned a kind of fearlessness that has enabled me to step out from the shadows and proclaim who I really am. I could even tell you that it has been an insanely powerful creative force in my life. But so what? These things may or may not be the results you find. All I can offer you is the question my meditation instructor asked me when I told him I was ready to commit to this path: "Are you ready for your whole life to change?"

May it bring you great benefit!

TWO

• • •

what meditation is

What is meditation anyway? Is it a path to peace? A means of transcendence? A way to connect with divine energies, destroy the ego (whatever that means), intuit answers to questions, discover the true meaning of life? Or is it simply a stress-reduction technique? The answer, of course, is "yes"—but, like most answers to profound questions, coming to a conclusion too quickly is a bad idea. The most important questions can only be answered in an intimate and nonconceptual way; such answers are received rather than cranked up. In other words, you will discover your own answer and it may or may not look like mine. In the meantime, here are some ideas to consider.

Meditation = simple substitution

When beginning a meditation practice, it is quite natural to have preconceived ideas. Perhaps you think it will remove all stresses from your life. Maybe you think you will be required to adopt foreign beliefs. Perhaps you hope it will help you with preexisting health concerns, solve relationship problems, or even turn you into the most compassionate person in the world, the Dalai Lama of Cleveland or Antwerp or Johannesburg. (Who knows? It might.)

Meditation could actually do all of these things, but the definition I'll offer you is very simple: all meditation is, is substituting for your discursive thoughts another object of attention.

That's it.

Let's break that down.

By "discursive thoughts" what I mean is that part of your mind that is always doing something like this:

What is she talking about I'll never be able to meditate Missy has been meditating for like six years and she is still an ass Maybe I should really, really do this every day Uh-oh I forgot to buy orange juice God I hope I don't get cancer I should really lose[gain] ten pounds If only I hadn't said that to him sixteen years ago . . .

And so on. I'm sure you know what I'm talking about. It goes on and on and such thoughts are most often the primary focus of our attention. They cascade end-lessly all day long, and sometimes all night long too.

I'm not saying there is anything wrong with these thoughts. They are quite normal. Many are uncomfortable, and some are completely brilliant; most, however, are pretty mundane.

To meditate, there is no need to stop these thoughts. It is really important to remember that and I will say more about it later.

In meditation, rather than allowing your mind to be thoughtlessly absorbed in thought (there is a koan for you), you purposely place it elsewhere. This may sound counterintuitive: like, *what are you supposed to think about if not your thoughts?* However, if you've ever

taken a long drive

gone to a yoga class

made out with someone

cooked a stew

solved a really difficult math problem

sketched a landscape

gone for a run or a swim

then you already know what is meant.

What do these disparate things have in common? Each requires you to place your mind on what you are doing rather than what you *think* about what you are doing. Each asks that you focus in a particular way. In fact, focus is necessary. In yoga, if you space out in tree pose, you might fall down. If you start thinking about lunch while trying to solve a complex math problem, you may lose a valuable line of thought. If you begin dreaming about your upcoming vacation while swimming, you may inhale water.

Activities like the ones on this list encourage the mind and body to be in the same place at the same time. This is extremely powerful. Meditation teachers call this "synchronizing mind and body."

Quite often, your mind and body are not synchronized, not at all. Your body lies down to sleep but your mind heads to the office. Your mind wants to finally write that novel but your body starts cleaning out closets. Your body is walking the boulevards of Paris but your mind is dreaming of swimming in Maui. Your mind should be focused on driving the car while your body is texting. (*Stop that, people!*) And so on. You get the idea.

This is all so exhausting. In fact, argument could be made that this and this alone—the splitting of mind and body—is actually at the root of the stress and fatigue many of us battle continuously. When mind and body are synchronized, we are in the present. In fact, that is all that is meant by "presence."

When we are present, interestingly, we relax. We enter a state of absorption. We are *right here* and somehow this right here—ness, though it might not always feel "good," feels alive. Powerful. Real.

By "relax," by the way, I don't mean "space out." I mean, "be with." Stop fighting. Stop trying to be anywhere else and just be right here. Sometimes this will feel great, sometimes it will feel uncomfortable or dull, and sometimes it will be just awful. Each instance is helpful because if we train only to stay with the happy parts of our experience, we will become quite small-minded and frightened. We are capable of so much more than this. (Positivity police, lay down your weapons!)

Rather than solving all your problems, then, meditation teaches you how to relax with them. When you are relaxed, amazing things happen. Self-confidence rises. You notice that emotional resilience is already present. Interesting insights emerge. You find that you are already strong and wise and flexible. You cheer up. This may sound like a fairy tale, but it is not.

In meditation, you synchronize mind and body by placing your focus on an object other than your discursive mind.

So, what is this object?

In some practices, that object is an image. You gaze at it (or visualize it in your mind's eye), and when your attention strays into discursiveness (Why am I doing this again? I wonder if her robe is made of brocade? I have so much to do. Is this even worthwhile?), you gently bring it back to the image. In other practices, that object is a sound, such as a mantra that you chant audibly or silently, and when your attention strays back into discursiveness (Why am I doing this again? What does OM even mean? I have so much to do. Is this even worthwhile?), you gently bring it back to the sound or sense of the mantra.

In the practice that I teach you in this book, that object of attention is your breath, which is quite conveniently located wherever you are. As you will see, you place your attention on the breath, and when it strays into discursiveness (Am I doing it right? I wonder if this is really how the Buddha attained enlightenment? I have so much to do. Is this even worthwhile?), you gently bring it back to the breath. It doesn't matter how many times you have to do so.

So, again: all meditation is, is substituting another object of attention for your discursive mind. While not easy, it is pretty simple. As you can see, it has nothing to do with trying to calm down or adopting foreign beliefs or figuring out whether God, gods, or goddesses exist or do not exist. All you have to do is sit down and breathe—and be very, very gentle toward yourself.

Interestingly, this last bit is perhaps the most difficult to do. Though we may start a meditation practice seeking peace and ease, the way we choose to get there may not support this search. We are pretty merciless toward ourselves. There is a lot of self-judgment, self-doubt, and even embarrassment about simply being who you are. We wield meditation as a kind of spiritual whip: *You're not doing it right, you know. You'll never figure it out, it's probably useless. Look how good Susie's posture is, you're a schlub compared to her. If you want this to work, you better try harder, much harder.* Perhaps unsurprisingly, beating ourselves up does not result in peace. It is thus of great importance to apply gentleness at every step of the practice, at the beginning, in the middle, and at the end.

A middle way

Often, people come to spiritual practice for one of two reasons that, on the face of it, appear contradictory. They are. In Buddhist thought, though, you don't have to choose either one. Instead, we opt for what is called the middle way.

The first group would like to gain access to more ethereal realms. There is a wish to transcend, to go elsewhere, to take up residence in a more perfect place, whether now or after death. People in this group would like the suffering and work of this life to garner either punishment or reward. Hopefully, someone really, really smart is deciding which. Having an inside line to this being is of great importance. Barring heavenly rewards, they may simply want to figure out a way to bliss out right here on earth.

The second group just wants to make life more bearable. They have no wish to probe the deeper meaning of their lives because they don't think there is one, and they're not wondering about what happens after death because what happens is nothing.

People in the first group may meditate for ecstasy and altered states of consciousness. Those in the second group just want to catch a break: get a good night's sleep, worry less, and generally not freak out so much.

There is nothing particularly wrong with either motivation—as long as we don't think that either one is absolutely correct.

There are certainly practices that promise eternal bliss in the hereafter. They could be called eternalistic.

There are prescriptive practices aimed at self-improvement without requiring acknowledgment of anything beyond what is concrete and measurable. This view could be called nihilistic.

Buddhist meditation does not embrace either position, nor, interestingly, does it refute them.

What are the other choices? You may be wondering.

Buddhism is sometimes described as the "middle way," and that means it is neither eternalistic nor nihilistic, but right down the middle. It's likely that in your practice you lean more toward one than the other. "I meditate to know God." Fine. Or, "That stuff is woo-woo. I meditate to lower my blood pressure." Also fine. Just don't think that either one is the point. The real point (if there is one) is, mysteriously, somewhere exactly in the middle.

Please enjoy contemplating this.

Mindfulness is only 50 percent of the story.

Often, meditation is called the practice of mindfulness, and that is fantastic, entirely accurate. However, it is only 50 percent of the story. Meditation consists of two inseparable qualities, only one of which is called "mindfulness."

The other one is called "awareness."

In meditation, as mentioned, we are asked to place our attention on the breath and, when it strays, to bring it back. I mean that quite seriously. Whether it strays into thoughts that are silly, beautiful, or dull, ideas that are important or life-changing, emotions that are irritating or powerful, the instruction remains the same: to *gently* let go and *gently* return your attention to the breath. That is how complete your one-pointedness should be. Breath. Breath. Breath. When one becomes absorbed in thought, it is not viewed as a problem but simply as beside the point. All you have to do is let go and begin again. And again and again and again. In this way, you develop focus, precision, and the ability to concentrate. This is what is meant by "mindfulness."

At the same time, however, from this one-pointedness, insight arises. As your meditation practice takes root, you see your life more clearly. You perceive patterns and connections you had not noticed before. Clarity and understanding seem to arise from nowhere. It feels as though your mind is expanding to point out that you exist in a much larger space than suspected; your perceptions become subtler and subtler. This is called "awareness."

The greater our ability to focus, the larger this awareness grows. The more aware we are, the more focused we can be. Mindfulness and awareness are inseparable.

So rather than calling meditation the practice of "mindfulness," it is more accurate to call it the practice of "mindfulness-awareness."

THREE

. . .

what meditation is not

It is not religious.

Meditation has nothing whatsoever to do with religion. No one has to adopt any new beliefs or swear allegiance to a deity to sit on this earth and breathe.

This concludes the section on what meditation is not.

FOUR

· · ·

common misconceptions

As mentioned, I've spoken to many people—friends, students, and fellow teachers—about meditation. I have had ample opportunity to notice (in myself and others) the misconceptions that we run into over and over again. For some reason, it is hard to let go of three misconceptions in particular and I want to point them out to you right up front.

To meditate, you have to stop thinking.

Actually, there *is* one thing you have to stop thinking—and it is that.

To meditate, you do not have to cease thought or "clear" the mind. In fact, that is a terrible idea. First of all, it is

vably frustrating. Part of your mind's job is to
thoughts and, you know, thank goodness. It's
just what the mind does and it's no problem. Instead of
trying to stop thinking, meditation is about assuming
a different relationship to your thoughts. Imagining
that you are going to sit down on the meditation cushion and pull some kind of spiritual emergency brake to
stop thought is misguided. Not to mention frustrating.
(I know I said that twice.)

I'd like to ask you to do a little experiment with me
that will demonstrate just how frustrating it is to stop
thinking. It will only take a few seconds.

Your eyes are open right now, yes? Look around.
Just look. Okay, got that?

Now: do it again but this time, *try not to see anything*.
Try really, really hard. Seriously.

That is how hard it is to stop thinking. Just as your
eyes exist to see things, your mind exists to produce
thoughts. Getting one or the other to stop is quite difficult, and even if you could, it would probably be terrifying, not to mention semi-pointless.

Now try another way. Look at one spot, but rather
than trying to focus on any one thing, allow the whole
visual field in. In other words, try to take in through
the eyes whatever is in their field without moving them
around. (It should feel like a softening of the eyes.)

Did you sense a shift in the quality of your vision
and what it felt like to see? If you did, notice what

it felt like. (If you didn't, you still get an A+. Don't worry about it; this simply may not be the best illustration for the way your beautiful mind works.)

This little exercise with the eyes demonstrates a better way to work with our thoughts. We can relax with the entire mental field by simply allowing what is there to be there. It is so much more relaxing than trying forcefully to ward off scary thoughts and hold tight to happy ones, which only creates a sense of failure and claustrophobia. Willfulness acts as an accelerant to thinking. Allowing is a decelerant.

Your mind is like a powerful freight train that runs up to speeds of a jillion miles per hour. Trying to stop it by leaping off the train and standing in front of it, waving your arms and going "Stop! Stop! Stop!" is, well, foolish. Instead of attempting to force the train to do our bidding, we simply hop off, take a comfortable seat on the grassy hillside, and watch it go by and by and by.

In addition to not having to cease thought, there is also no call to think only happy thoughts, positive thoughts, or attractive thoughts. Your mind can be exactly as it is: cheerful, tranquil, sublime, dull, trivial, barbaric, tumultuous, bleak. It can all be brought into the practice. Nothing need be excluded. In this way, you make room for the full power of your mind to manifest. To open in this way is a fierce gesture of creative courage, one that is worthy of you, rather than the small-mindedness of fearing your thoughts. Suddenly, we see that we live in a much bigger and more beautiful space than we may have ever dreamed. Some parts are elegant and rich while others are broken and shrouded. You can walk among it all with complete grace. There is nothing to fear, nothing whatsoever.

Meditation is a form of self-improvement.

Okay, okay, it *will* improve your life. But it goes so much further than that.

Meditation is a precious opportunity to untether yourself from the self-improvement treadmill that many of us ride so hard. Your practice is a time to stop trying to be a better anything and instead release all agendas and relax with yourself just as you are. You don't need to become a bigger, better, skinnier, fatter, smarter, richer version of you, and if you enlist your meditation practice in the service of self-improvement, it will lose its magic. You are already exactly who you want to be. Meditation is a way of clearing up any confusion about this, but it works on you in mysteriously nonlinear ways. Rather than trying to make yourself perfect, you relax into your natural perfection. The practice opens itself to you and takes you on a journey that is far more interesting than what you may have imagined. When we let the practice guide us rather than dictating its direction, the magic takes hold.

Meditation makes you into a peaceful person.

I was tempted to write "ha ha ha ha," but I didn't want to be too flip. And, really, in some ways it *does* make you more peaceful, just not in the ways you may expect.

It often happens with my meditation students (as happened with me) that they say, "The more I practice, the more emotional I feel. I'm not becoming more quote-unquote peaceful, I'm actually becoming more vulnerable. What am I doing wrong?"

Now we get to a little secret about meditation practice. It does not make you more peaceful, if by peaceful you mean unflappable or unperturbed or some other kind of state where everything is always okay and nothing ever bothers you.

Rather than creating an inner environment that is akin to a still pond (which can only remain so if the wind never blows or a leaf never drops or the temperature never shifts or a fish never swims in it), your practice drops you into a deep part of the sea, a place that sometimes sparkles peacefully and at others roils as if blown by the winds of hell. It reveals you to be the waveform that is capable of all these different manifestations and that has no option but to eventually be reabsorbed into stillness. This is you. *This* is you. This "you" is so much bigger than having to choose between each little thought as either for or against you.

You find that you don't have to be afraid of yourself. *And then you soften.* This is where everything begins to change. The defenses that you constructed so carefully, to protect what you now see may not be in need of such protection, begin to come down. With lowered walls, what you once held at bay—your sadness or anger, the joy or sorrow of those you love, the tremendous brilliance and cruelty of our world—comes in. You are more easily touched. You laugh and cry more easily. This is a very good sign. It is not, however, synonymous with peace. I submit that it is something even better.

Rather than becoming more peaceful, meditation makes you more *authentic.*

FIVE

. . .

kinds of meditation

Recently I was on Google+ when I saw a post from a
new meditator about how hard it was to meditate and
how easily he became distracted. What should he do?
He got all kinds of advice from the Google+ meditation community. Some people suggested he seek
greater isolation. Some urged him to rid himself of defilements in order to transcend conventional concerns.
Some thought he should just try harder. I suggested
that he relax.

Each of these suggestions has merit.

Certain meditation practices emphasize austerity and
renunciation, and thus seeking greater isolation would
make sense.

Other practices focus on waking up to the true nature of reality and hold that "defilements" or mistaken views prevent this—and so urging purification is a kindly suggestion.

There are practices that recognize laziness as the primary obstacle to meditation and so "try harder" is a way to neutralize this tendency.

Still other practices see meditation as a path to compassion and love and suggest that these qualities arise spontaneously when we let down our guard. That is where my suggestion to relax came from.

Obviously, none of these directions are wrong. In fact they are all right—however, depending on your point of view (and your karma), one is most likely to be right for *you*.

How to discover which?

I am happy to offer a few suggestions for parsing the vast world of meditative practices, but a few caveats are in order.

First, the only practices I can comment on are those connected to Buddhism. I know there are a vast array of other practices, some that are associated with ancient wisdom traditions and some that are newfangled and culturally current—but all of my experience is within the world of the Buddhadharma and I wouldn't presume to comment on anything outside of that.

Second, within the world of Buddhism, my experience belongs exclusively to one tradition among thousands. I have only practiced in the Shambhala Buddhist lineage, which is a Tibetan school. I have practiced *za-zen*, but only a few times when I taught a program at a Zen center. I have never practiced *vipassana* (probably the most well-known in the West of the Buddhist meditation styles), although I know many vipassana teachers and, well, some of my best friends are vipassana practitioners. Additionally, I know only the most basic facts about mindfulness-based stress reduction (MBSR), the powerful mindfulness practice that has been accepted as part of many healthcare treatment protocols. Among the most popular Buddhist schools in North America is the Nichiren school, they who chant NAM MYOHO RENGE KYO, about which I know virtually nothing.

There are other styles—many, countless other styles—of which I have no knowledge as they remain cloistered within whatever cultural group claims them. But I will not let any of this stand in our way!! In this chapter, I'll offer you some insights into the differences and similarities between the most well-known Buddhist meditation styles in the West, and in the Resources section (Appendix C) I provide some links if you want to pursue further information. Please just bear in mind that my view is colored by my experience. If you asked a vipassana or Zen teacher to explain the various styles, they would surely say something other than what I say below.

There is yet one more thought for you to contemplate. It's an important one.

It is very tempting to think that all meditation styles are essentially the same and simply present a variety of roads to arrive at a single destination. Thus, whatever one you choose will be fine. This is not so. The spiritual path is different for everyone. Different paths proscribe different means for discovering what it might mean to *you*. They don't all go in the same direction, or at least they don't move at the same speed or via the same means. The practice that is right for you is right for you specifically. Of course there may be millions of others for whom it is also right, but that actually has no bearing—selecting one practice is a very personal and intimate decision that no one can tell you how to make. Thus, the most important thing to remember about settling on a particular practice is to follow your heart. You may try a variety of practices (and I hope you will) until you experience one that makes you think, "Aha. Finally something that makes sense." That is a good clue. In the meantime, let your practice be a tad promiscuous. They can all be friends with benefits. However, as with relationships, if you want to get serious, you're going to have to commit. Commitment is best as a follow-up to falling in love. This is the only way to deepen the practice beyond conceptual mind and conventional wisdom, both of which I'm sure have great qualities. Nonetheless, your original mind and outrageous wisdom lie just beyond the pale of what you currently think, all puns intended.

Okay. Enough caveats.

1. *Shamatha*, or "the practice of tranquillity," is the practice I am most familiar with and it is also the style that I teach. I go into great detail on shamatha in chapter 7, so I'm not going to say too much about it here beyond that I teach it in a way that is associated with my Tibetan lineages. It is a practice of calming and focusing your mind through placement of attention on the breath.

2. Vipassana, or "the practice of insight," is the practice of expanding awareness to include not only the breath but also whatever else might be arising, including sounds, bodily sensations, and general changes in the atmosphere. Traditionally, it is associated with Theravada, the oldest surviving branch of Buddhism. Many of the most respected and well-known Western dharma teachers have roots in the Theravada, which emphasizes, among many things, the practice of vipassana. These teachers, most notably Tara Brach, Joseph Goldstein, Jack Kornfield, and Sharon Salzberg, have done much to translate traditional Buddhist teachings for Western students by honoring the heart essence of the practice while stripping away Eastern cultural trappings.

3. Mindfulness meditation or mindfulness-based stress reduction was developed primarily by Jon Kabat-Zinn,

a medical doctor who introduced meditation as a therapeutic means to treat a variety of medical conditions. He has done a brilliant job of presenting meditation free of religious connotations. Though Kabat-Zinn was originally trained in the Zen tradition, MBSR utilizes a technique called the "body scan," which is connected to vipassana.

4. Zazen is the central practice for many forms of Zen Buddhism. It is the practice of sitting quietly and letting all thoughts, sensations, images, ideas, and emotions go by to "just sit." It is most often practiced in an atmosphere of simplicity, rigor, and directness that encourages disciplined adherence to the zazen technique.

Though there are differences between the various Buddhist practices, you could say that each emphasizes in varying degrees these three attributes: precision, openness, and going beyond.

Precision means choosing a particular object of attention and staying with it, holding your attention to it as best you can. When attention strays, the instruction is simply to bring it back. *Everything that is not that object is considered a distraction.* In other words, if the object of your attention is your breath and you find yourself lost in thought about lunch or the probability that you will get cancer (or that your bank balance will), you let those thoughts go to return attention to breath.

If there is noise in the next room, you notice it (how can you not?), let it go, and return attention to breath.

If you find that anger has arisen at something your partner said two minutes or two decades ago, you let both the thought and the feeling go.

If you find that you are thinking about your breath and how awesome you are (or are not) at focusing on it, you let that go too.

You don't banish or ignore these other objects of attention that are not your breath; you simply let go of them in the same way you would notice and let go of a Mötley Crüe song that started running through your mind as you were trying to listen to a Bach cello concerto. Later, Vince Neil. You are not the point right now.

This degree of precision cultivates the precious, profound, and increasingly rare ability to *concentrate*. When you can place your attention where you'd like it to go, you find yourself in possession of an authentic superpower, mental kryptonite of the highest order. You are able to be mindful. This is actually what "mindfulness" means—the ability to place your attention (or mind) on what you choose.

Practices that emphasize mindfulness are potent indeed and tend to encourage qualities such as discipline, clarity, and commitment.

Openness is something that naturally arises from mindfulness. Somehow, as we cultivate the ability to place and hold our attention at will, our mind expands. Insights arise. We see connections we missed before. Things we didn't understand become clear. "Gut" feelings are stronger. I really don't know how concentration gives rise to greater awareness, but according to practitioners over many millennia (and my own personal experience), it does.

The willingness to pay attention to what is currently happening (rather than *our thoughts* about what is currently happening) means opening to what is. Usually, we stick to our thoughts about what is: "this is good, that is bad, I like this, I don't like that, this makes me happy, this frightens me" and so on.

Letting go of this steady commentary from moment to moment, we open up.

When we open up, we see and feel things we hadn't before. Awareness expands. A kind of freshness and tenderness permeates the atmosphere.

Perhaps because of this, practices that emphasize awareness tend to also focus on compassion and love.

The third component, going beyond, is perhaps the most inscrutable and difficult to quantify.

To practice precision and openness, we find that we must continually let go. The moment we hold on—to a thought, feeling, conclusion, opinion—we have taken ourselves outside the flow of the present moment. To remain present, we notice and let go almost simultaneously. *At first, this is very odd.* We feel groundless because we are constantly giving up the "certainty" of what we think, feel, need, hope for, and fear in order to remain mindful and aware.

The truth is, whatever you think, feel, and so on, is constantly changing. When you examine this closely, you might see that there actually is no solid state of mind. Though we have spent all our lives cultivating the ground of personality, identity, and belief, these actually are not solid, not the whole picture.

So what is real, then? Well, I don't know how to answer that definitively, but we could start by recognizing that groundlessness is real. We aren't anchored anywhere because there is no place to put down.

Through consistently (and at times, abruptly) releasing all fixity of mind, practices that focus on going beyond also stress recognition that the nature of all phenomena is empty and luminous.

It is worth noting that these three qualities—precise, open, and going beyond—are not sequential and there is no need to choose from among them. They are actually inseparable. When you cultivate one, you are also seeding the ground for the other two. It is not unusual, however, for different traditions to place primary emphasis on one of these qualities to begin with. (Which is fine. All roads lead to nowhere.) For example, one practice may encourage absolute adherence to the meditation technique with no alterations or gaps of any kind. That is great, and for those of us who tend to be too loosey-goosey anyway, may be the perfect practice. Other practices may place more importance on lightening up, and this can be great for those of us who are already too hard on ourselves.

These three components of precision, openness, and going beyond mirror the three major schools, or *yanas*, of Buddhism.

SIX

• • •

three yanas

It is said that the Buddha "turned the wheel of dharma" three times, or or gave three main cycles of teachings, which create the three yanas of Buddhism. (Some say that the last two are actually a single cycle. But I digress.) *Yana* means "vehicle," and each teaching cycle is meant as a fully outfitted conveyance to get you from Point A to Point Enlightenment.

The first cycle of teachings belongs to the Hinayana, which could be translated as "foundational vehicle." These are the very first teachings of the Buddha, given upon his enlightenment in response to people's curiosity about what he saw at the moment of liberation. They focus on the critical basics for anyone beginning on the path to enlightenment.

If you want to become enlightened, you have to start with your actual life, just as it is right now, and begin by getting your personal situation in hand. Hinayana teachings are concerned with nailing the basics: not killing, not lying, not becoming a drunkard, and so on. Further, they encourage you to renounce what can reasonably be called "all the bullshit": money, fame, success, and so on. (It's not that there is anything wrong with those things, as long as you don't think they will make you happy. They only become problems when you imagine they might.)

To accomplish these practices, it helps to keep your life very, very simple and temptations to a minimum; after all, most of us will need to renounce the bullshit on more than one occasion. The Hinayana counsels a life of discipline—not the onerous, punishing kind, but the kind that can actually create a life of joy. Little slips are to be avoided because they really seem to pile up. Rather than being seen as moral wrongdoings, however, they are seen as obstacles and obscurations to true wakefulness and as such are to be eschewed. To do so, tremendous precision is required. I mean, take just one of the most basic precepts, common to every religion under the sun: "don't lie." If you can read to the end of this paragraph without telling a lie, please alert the media. I'm not insinuating that you are a liar, dear reader. I'm just saying that when you closely observe the emails you write, the phone messages you leave, the casual banter with a colleague—the most mundane interactions with others—you will find a ton of small and basically inconsequential "lies." Forget about what you'll find if you look at your responses during more intense interactions where you may want to look good, get your way, or get off the hook. Forget further about what you see when you examine your own thoughts for truthfulness. Even the simple instruction "don't lie," then, is enormously complex. Unbelievable presence of mind is required to follow it.

The second cycle is the Mahayana, which means "greater vehicle." It is not called this because it is better. (Hinayana practitioners can get very mad if you think it does, and rightfully so.) I like to think that it is called "greater" because the teachings of the Mahayana take you beyond your personal situation and ask you to take your place in the greater world. They take the focus off of your personal behavior and place it on the way you relate to the people around you and also the way you relate to space. During this cycle, the teachings focus on what we need to know once we have gotten our personal life somewhat together—meaning, we have a home, food, livelihood, friends, and so on. Under these circumstances, something very wonderful happens naturally. Your heart blossoms open to others. Further, these teachings focus on recognizing the illusory nature of, well, everything.

When you look at others from a place of confidence about your own life, they appear as potentially lovable beings. When you look at them from a place of need or uncertainty, they appear as potential devices for good or ill in your happiness schemes. (Others tend not to care for this.) So the Mahayana teachings are very much about love and compassion in both of their forms: relative and absolute.

On the relative plane, love and compassion are what we might expect them to be: acting kindly, thinking of others, and so forth. (For more on the complexity of compassion, see chapter 17, "Meditation and Compassion.")

On the absolute plane, love and compassion manifest as emptiness. Please contemplate on your own what this could mean, as to delve into it would take us far beyond the confines of this work, not to mention the galaxy. Plus, I don't really understand it. However, in both the relative and absolute states, compassion is seen as a kind of opening.

The third cycle of teachings is the Vajrayana, or "indestructible vehicle." Sometimes it is translated as the "adamantine" or "diamond" vehicle. These teachings focus on what you might concern yourself with once your personal life and your heart are in a settled state: viewing every moment of your life as a chance to wake up to the true nature of reality and what might happen after that. The Vajrayana, or Tantric path, contains

Buddhism's esoteric teachings on the journey to enlightenment. It is associated with practices such as Dzogchen ("The Great Perfection") and Mahamudra ("The Great Seal"). To walk this path requires continual letting go of concepts, ideas, judgments, and thoughts and plunging yourself into a state of groundlessness and, with the support of a teacher, stabilizing yourself there.

Each of these dharma cycles is unspeakably profound. Each cycle has a progression of teachings and practices that range from beginner to advanced and beyond. Each cycle can claim great teachers of the most profound and enlightened sort. Each cycle can show you how to become enlightened. You can enter through any doorway but no one can tell you which one is right for you. It is a highly personal decision.

Finally, one might say that the cycles are not progressive; rather, they are circular.

The Hinayana took root in many places but is currently found mostly in Southeast Asia: in Cambodia, Thailand, and so on. The Mahayana teachings inform most of the styles of Buddhism in China (where it is known as Chan) and Japan (where it is called Zen.) The Vajrayana took root in a much smaller area: in fact, a tiny area, relatively speaking. The Vajrayana has been practiced almost exclusively in Tibet and Bhutan.

My training is as a student of the Vajrayana. I know almost nothing about schools outside of the Vajrayana, about which I know next to nothing. Please believe me when I say that I am not being self-deprecating. I have been a practitioner for close to twenty years, and if I can tell you one thing about the dharma with absolute certainty, it is this: it is vast beyond my capacity to imagine. The more I learn, the less I realize that I know. I don't say this to be discouraging, but to let you know how profound and sweeping these teachings are: every time I think that I understand the inner meaning of one teeny-tiny corner of one teeny-tiny teaching, in that very moment the teaching itself gives way to reveal itself as far deeper than I had guessed. It's like opening a door to what you thought was a closet to find that it actually opens out onto the sky.

Within Tibetan Buddhism, there are four main schools: Nyingma, Kagyu, Geluk, and Sakya. Within each of these, there are many subsets. And this is just the Vajrayana. Within the Hinayana and Mahayana there are many more such subsets, as these schools are practiced by far more people and have a longer history.

To close the loop on my particular lineage, Shambhala Buddhism (which is one of the first schools to have arisen in the West), I will tell you that its progenitor, Chögyam Trungpa (the aforementioned), held lineages in both the Nyingma and Kagyu schools.

I'm sure that I will mention Chögyam Trungpa and his son, Sakyong Mipham (who is the current head of Shambhala and is my teacher), many times throughout this book. I love and admire them both and each has transformed my life: Trungpa through his books and Sakyong Mipham through direct teachings.

That said, I am in no way attempting to sway you that the Vajrayana is the coolest yana or that Chögyam Trungpa or Sakyong Mipham are the best teachers. Naturally, I think they are, but I hope that you will find who and what *you* think is best.

And just in case you're thinking that the Vajrayana must be the highest because, well, for whatever reason you may have, the last public talk Chögyam Trungpa gave before he passed away in 1987 literally consisted of one line, "Never forget the Hinayana." Though I was not there, I think of this often. It points not only to the inseparability of the yanas, but to the overarching importance of beginning with (and constantly returning to) the discipline of precision.

SEVEN

• • •

how to choose

How do you know which practice is right for you? I mean, there are so many varieties being promoted. Some promise stress reduction. Some promise transcendence. Some promise enlightenment. Some promise nothing, while others promise everything: peace, bliss, weight loss, powers of attraction.

How can you tell the meritorious from the cheesy? I offer you these suggestions:

1. Choose a practice that is rooted in a lineage that is older than, oh, twenty-five hundred years. Not saying you have to adopt another culture or act all Eastern, just that it's good to find something time-tested and honed. Thus you can have confidence—and confi-

dence is always step one along the spiritual path. Avoid practices that someone made up last week or last decade or that sample various wisdom traditions to create an amalgam. Stick with what is real.

2. Learn the technique from someone who has been trained to teach it. Teaching meditation is more than an explanation, it is a transmission. It is passed down from one who has learned from his teacher, who learned from her teacher, and so on. The longer the chain, in some sense, the greater the power of the practice. If your friend is all psyched about the meditation she is doing and wants to teach it to you, great. But don't stop there. If you like it, go to the source she learned it from and get instruction from a teacher.

3. Don't accept anything watered down or instant. There are many skillful and intelligent ways to present the practice simply and I'm not referring to any such attempts. It's just that meditation takes effort and will at some point be uncomfortable and boring. Any practice that promises otherwise should be investigated especially carefully. Stay away from things that can be done in five, seven, or zero steps. It's just not that simple.

4. Don't make stuff up. This is one area of life where it's really important to get the instruction, contemplate it carefully, and then follow it closely. At some point in your practice maybe you'll figure out some personal

tweaks to the technique. But hold all tweaks for months, years, even lifetimes. The thing with practices that are rooted and long-lasting is that they are soaked in wisdom. They've seen all the pranks we play to avoid actually looking at our own minds. Thus, while there is no need to be heavy-handed, no detail is casual. It's all there for a reason. Respect and love the technique and it will respect and love you back.

5. At the same time, whatever practice you choose will only come to life when you make it very personal. There are wonderful guides who can help you enter the practice, and maybe at some point you will even find a Teacher or Guru. In any case, at every step you are still charged with bringing what you have learned into your own life. You have got to figure it out yourself. Don't take anyone's word for anything. Trust, verify. Trust, verify. Repeat. Your experience *is* the path; there is no other path. So stick with practices that encourage deep inward looking and personal responsibility while respecting tradition and venerating that tradition's masters.

6. Unless you have a really compelling reason, avoid practices that suggest that the point is bliss. Or transcendence. Personally, I don't want to go somewhere else; I want to be right *here*. I'd like to experience my actual life before heading off to explore another sphere. And no one even knows what bliss is, anyway. I don't.

All I know is that it's something other than feeling super-happy and unencumbered. (When asked what bliss felt like, Chögyam Trungpa said, "To you, it would probably feel like pain.") Practice should make you more human, not less. It introduces you to the brilliant, confused, grumpy, joyful, and deeply tender person that you already are and opens door after door for this amazing being (you) to enter the phenomenal world—for her benefit, yes, but also for the benefit of all sentient beings. The point of the practice, one could say, is just this: to help each other. Practices that leave this part out or sequester it as a natural side effect of your personal happiness skeeve me out a bit.

Of course, my opinion is that my lineage of Shambhala Buddhism fits all these parameters and so I recommend it. I also heartily recommend the practices associated with other schools of Tibetan Buddhism, as well as Zen and vipassana (or insight meditation). But whatever you choose should obviously do more than fit a list of qualifications. We're talking about your spiritual path, here! Look for something you can fall in love with. Heart connection with a lineage, teacher, or community trumps everything I just said.

So definitely try things out. However, at some point it is important to choose one path (or no path—this is best for some folks) and stay with that way.

EIGHT

• • •

our practice: shamatha

Now that you have heard my long, one-sided, cursory explanation of the various meditation styles, where they are (loosely) affiliated, and guidelines for selecting one, I'm going to introduce you to the kind of meditation I teach and that we will be practicing together as part of this book.

I was taught to meditate by my meditation instructor on one memorable day in 1993. Sometime in the 1970s, he was taught by his teacher, Chögyam Trungpa, who was taught, presumably, by his teacher (sometime in the 1940s or 1950s), who was taught by his teacher, who was taught by his teacher, and so on, all the way back to the Buddha. I'm not pointing this out to make you think I'm standing in for the Buddha, but so that you can know that when I give you the instruction, there is an unbroken line of transmission. There is something about this through-line that is important.

As mentioned previously, the practice I teach is called shamatha meditation. *Shamatha* is a Sanksrit word that is translated variously as "the practice of peacefully abiding" or "the practice of tranquillity." Shamatha is said to have been taught by the Buddha himself more than twenty-five hundred years ago. It has been practiced by countless individuals over the millennia, and there is a tremendous body of knowledge about how this practice can create and sustain balance, even in a speedy, out-of-control world.

Which is awesome. We are all seeking a tranquil place where we can abide peacefully. Sometimes the wish to get away can be quite urgent, and we may think that to do so, we have to go to the beach, call in sick, or take a long drive. However, there is a place where you can always abide peacefully, and that is within your own mind.

I realize this may sound strange because the one thing we want to avoid when stressed is our thoughts. If we could only just shut out our worries and fears for a little while, we could regroup and reenter our lives with a bit more energy.

That works—it is true. Getting away from it all is fantastic, and if you've ever taken a real vacation, you know how much perspective and vibrancy you gain and how keenly you want to hold on to it when vacation time is over. So, yes, getting away from stressors is definitely one way to relax.

But there is another way. Rather than getting away from it all to relax, you could relax in the midst of it all. You could relax with what makes you happy, and you could relax with what makes you sad, irritable, frustrated, excited, angry, and so on. This turns out to be far more pragmatic than booking a trip to Cancun every time you get freaked out.

By "relax with," I don't mean space out, ignore, or remain unaffected by. I mean, "allow." Once you start to pay attention (as meditation teaches you to), you will see that your difficult emotions are 10 percent agitation and 90 percent cogitation. In other words, it is our thoughts that cause more distress than anything.

I'll give you an example. My last book was called *The Wisdom of a Broken Heart* and it is about how to relate with that most painful of emotional states, heartbreak. Though this book was written in recent years, the inspiration for it arose close to two decades ago when I was suffering with my own broken heart. It was awful. There was one particular point where it began to turn around and I recall the exact moment, and I mean precisely, down to the second, when it happened because when it did, I heard a voice.

I was living in Austin, Texas, at the time. My boyfriend and I had broken up a zillion times because we had different approaches to life but always got back together because we loved each other a lot. During one of our breakups, he started seeing another woman and, really, I can't explain why even all these years later and after having written an entire *book* on the topic, I fell apart. My world collapsed. I was utterly, thoroughly broken. Bereft. On fire with grief and longing. (If you've ever gone through such a breakup, you know exactly what I am talking about.) I couldn't eat. I couldn't sleep. I thought about him, me, him and her, me and him, us, myself, them, all day long and all night long too. It seemed that the moment my head hit the pillow, I would begin to dream about them, together, laughing, ignoring me. Though these nightmares had all of the emotional subtlety of a children's cartoon, *they tormented my soul*. I would wake up crying and then go back to sleep, falling right into the exact moment where the last nightmare had left off, like it was waiting for me to come back. Oh, oh, oh. It seemed my sorrow would never end.

One day I was taking the trash out because, well, it was trash day. I lived in a house that sat atop a little hill. I was wheeling the garbage cans down to the curb, basically oozing salt water. I was sobbing. I was sweating. (It was Texas in the summer.) My mind would not let me go and the rate at which obsessive thoughts were firing sped faster and faster. *I hate him. I hate myself. I hate her. I hate them. I hate everyone. I will never love again, I am such an idiot. No, he is an idiot and she is an asshole. I will never love again and I will die lonely. He didn't deserve me and he is going to be so sorry and if only I hadn't worn pink to that party or answered the phone last Sunday, none of this would be happening,* and so on, etcetera, ad nauseam. By the time I got to the curb, I was crying so hard that I could barely stand up and so I sat down between the garbage cans and thought, maybe when the trash people come, they won't realize I'm not trash and will throw me away too because I don't think I can take this anymore. *I CAN'T TAKE IT ANYMORE.*

In that moment, hand to god, I heard a voice. I have no idea where it came from. It said, "But nothing is happening right now." This notion took me by surprise. I stopped. I looked around. It was true. Nothing was happening. No one was taunting me. No one was denying or affirming my greatness. My ex and his new girlfriend weren't there, laughing and pointing. *Nothing was happening.* It was trash day in Austin. I could feel the heat of the curb through my cutoffs. I could hear the noise of traffic a few streets over. That's it. There was no heartbreak, nothing lost, nothing gained, no torment, and no liberation from torment. I was just sitting there. *I was free.* Upon recognizing this, I felt a tremendous, life-altering surge of pure liberation that lasted for, oh, nine seconds. (Nine *awesome* seconds.) Then it all came pouring back. But I never forgot that nine-second gap when I realized that it wasn't the circumstances of my life that were causing most of my pain, it was my thoughts. If I could learn to work with my thoughts, it stood to reason, I could heal my heart.

This turned out to be true. Although I didn't discover this until I began Buddhist meditation practice some years later, I learned that the trick was not to replace icky thoughts with pleasing thoughts, as in, "I do deserve love! I am great! People love me! I'm super rich and happy!" and so forth—affirmations that Pema Chödrön describes as "like screaming that you're okay in order to overcome this whisper that you're not." Such thoughts actually amp up agitation. Nor was it helpful (or even possible) to push away my thoughts or forget about them or argue myself out of them. It didn't even help all that much to try to explain them. I mean, no matter how thorough and precise an explanation you craft for why pain hurts, it still just hurts. So what is left?

What is left is to relax with your thoughts and feelings just as they are. You could notice your thoughts and feel your feelings. When you get carried away by what comes next—the story attached to those thoughts and feelings—you could let go of it and return to a simple state of acknowledgment and feeling. It turns out that this is the key to metabolizing experiences of all kinds. Who knew.

The ability to make space for what you think and feel has enormous implications. You can have patience with the creative process, because you don't bail the second doubt arises and you tell yourself you have no talent, who wants to read your writing anyway, what right do you have to call yourself an artist, and so on. (I have heard tell of such thoughts.) You can tolerate the discomfort of not knowing what is going to happen when you quit your job to start your own business. When the one you love tells you she loves you back, you can actually appreciate that genuinely. When she tells you she doesn't, you have a way to meet the pain. You can actually show up for your own life.

Notice I did not say that when you learn how to relax with yourself you can avoid doubt, discomfort, rage, or sorrow. Right here is where a lot of confusion about meditation arises. It is not about avoiding your life; it is about living it fully. It is not about becoming implacable, it is about becoming genuine.

That is what our practice is about.

NINE

• • •

how to meditate

Find a comfortable place to sit. If you can sit on a meditation cushion, that's great. If this is too uncomfortable for any reason, it's fine to sit on a chair. It's helpful to designate a particular spot for meditation, so, if possible, choose a particular room or corner of a room to establish your practice. Make your sitting area pleasant. If you wish, you could sit in front of a shelf or table with some cherished or beautiful objects on them, like fresh flowers, some river stones, or a picture of someone or something you love. Keep it simple. The idea is to create a spot that you feel good about returning to.

There are three aspects to pay attention to in meditation practice.

Body

The practice begins with how you take your seat. Meditation posture is actually quite specific. Simply sit up straight, not rigidly, but in a relaxed, upright position. The main thing to remember is to *feel* yourself in your body, not outside of it, judging your posture as correct or incorrect. (I sometimes feel as though I am hovering around or just outside of my body, hoping I might be able to ignore it somehow.) The practice actually begins when you "land." You could feel that as your sit bones reach down into the earth, the crown of your head reaches slightly up, as if some kind and gentle person had put his palm a few centimeters above it and you would like to touch it. Imagine yourself as a tree whose roots are planted in the ground, but that also sways and moves with the wind. In this way, your posture should be firmly planted but also supple. When you sit upright like this, you are proclaiming your dignity.

If you are seated on a cushion, cross your legs loosely in front of you. Some people prefer to have their knees lower than the hips, some higher. Play around and see what works for you.

Some people feel most comfortable with only a very thin cushion to elevate their hips; others require a cushion that is one or two feet high. You may have to experiment with cushion heights to find the right setup for yourself.

If you are on a chair, scoot forward so that your back is not resting on anything and your feet are flat on the floor. For most people who meditate sitting in a chair, it's nice to have the knees a little higher than the hips. To accomplish this, place a cushion under your feet.

When you've found a comfortable posture, place your hands, palms down, just above your knees or at mid-thigh. Let your shoulders and belly relax.

Tuck your chin a little bit so that the back of the neck is long. Your mouth should be closed, with the lips slightly parted, tongue resting on the roof of the mouth. Let the jaw relax.

In this practice, the eyes remain open. The gaze is soft and cast slightly down, to a spot about six feet in front of you. (Or a couple of meters if you are in a meter country.) It's not like you're staring at that spot or at anything in particular—it's more like vision is streaming out from your eyes and mixing with space instead of targeting anything in particular. Although they are open, your eyes are relaxed with the sense that they are sitting back in their sockets, as opposed to straining forward. It doesn't matter what your gaze comes to rest on; just let it settle on a spot six feet in front.

Breath

Once you have established your posture, begin to notice the rise and fall of your breath. Feel yourself breathing. Decisively *be* with your breath. Each breath is different. Can you tell how? Breathe naturally. Allow attention to ride the breath like waves in the ocean.

Placing awareness on the breath is different from thinking about the breath. Here is a simple demonstration of what is meant by placement of attention. Without moving or looking, right now allow your awareness to settle around your right big toe. Allow yourself simply to become conscious of that little piggy. Notice if it feels squished or snug in your sock, or if you can feel the air around it. Now, also without moving or looking, move your awareness to your left ear lobe. Again, just notice it hanging out there in space. Maybe it's adorned with an earring, perhaps it's covered by your hair. Now move awareness back to the right big toe. And again up to the left ear lobe.

Whatever just moved is your attention. That is what you place on the breath in meditation.

Mind

At some point, you may notice that your attention has drifted away from the breath and become absorbed in thought. That is absolutely no problem, none whatsoever. Often, I hear people say things like, "I tried to meditate but I couldn't stop thinking! There's no way I can do it." But there is no need to stop thinking, only to develop a different relationship to your thoughts. When thoughts arise, simply notice them and allow them to float by. Keep your attention on your breath. When a particular thought absconds with your attention, as soon as you notice this, just let it go and return attention to breath. It doesn't matter how long you've been "gone." The important thing is to come back. Gently let the thought ease away like a wave eases back into the ocean. It doesn't matter how wonderful, horrendous, boring, creative, or critically insightful your thought has been. Just let go.

When it comes to thoughts, let them touch you and then flow away, as if you were standing barefoot in a stream and occasional leaves or pebbles momentarily brushed up against you and then were gone. In meditation, thoughts are also famously equated to clouds in the sky. Some are cheerful and bright while some seem to bear ominous portent. Some are fat and fluffy and beautiful and others are barely perceptible beyond a far-off streak of white. Sometimes clouds block the sky altogether. But you know that just beyond them, the sun is always shining, clear and bright. The meditation researcher and practitioner Jon Kabat-Zinn says that in meditation practice, instead of identifying with the clouds, we identify ourselves as the sky. The sky doesn't care what kind of clouds pass through or how long they stay. And, just like the sky, we can hold it all and know that no matter what direction we happen to be facing, somewhere it is always east and somewhere the sun is always rising.

Mindfulness of body can create a sense of stability. Mindfulness of breath creates a sense of peace. And mindfulness of mind creates a sense of tremendous spaciousness. Together, mindfulness of body, breath, and mind create your meditation practice.

TEN

• • •

tips for establishing your practice

When you have established your body, breath, and mind in the practice of meditation, try to sit for around ten minutes per day. It's better to sit for a short period every day than a longer period on some days. Consistency is more important than duration. It is better to practice for ten minutes per day, five days a week, than for fifty minutes, one day a week.

Start slowly.

Don't say to yourself: "I am going to meditate every single day for the rest of my life." This is a big mistake—first, because you're not, and second, because it's just too much pressure. That is like beginning a running practice by starting with a half marathon. Instead, establish a routine that is very, very doable. For example, you could decide to meditate Monday through Friday for ten minutes per day. For one month. That would be great. At the end of that month, decide whether you want to continue with ten-minute sessions, slow down, or increase the time. If you want to increase, do so by small increments—say, five minutes. Then, after a month of sitting for fifteen minutes, you can make a decision for the succeeding time period.

Establish your seat.

You don't have to create anything fancy or spend a lot of money, but choose one place for your practice—either a corner of your bedroom or office, a particular chair in your living room, or, if you live in a mansion, an entire room. Choose a spot that you enjoy being in. Keep it clean and tidy. If you like, you could have a small offering table with flowers or a picture of someone or something that inspires you. Don't get carried away here, though. Keep it simple.

Find a timer of some sort. You could use an alarm clock or a stick of incense. (If you like incense, burn a stick and time how long it takes to finish. If it takes twenty minutes to burn completely and you've decided to practice for twenty minutes, you're in great shape. If you've decided on ten minutes, stop practicing when it's halfway burned.) If you'd like, you can light a candle or place a photo of something or someone inspiring nearby, but these things are not necessary.

Choose your time.

Try to practice at the same time every day. Most people find that the morning works out best, but you may have a dozen kids to get off to school or a job that requires your presence at 6 A.M. Or you may simply be a night owl and find it better to practice when you get home from work or just before bed. You can experiment with times of day, but whatever seems best, stick with it. There is nothing magical about this; it just seems that habits thrive on routine.

Declare your intention.

As you sit down to practice, say to yourself something like this: *Now is my time to practice. Everything else can wait.* Commit yourself at the outset.

Follow the twelve-second rule.

This rule states that when you screw up (i.e., miss a day or a week or a month on the cushion), you must feel awful, guilty, and ashamed—but only for twelve seconds!! Then you have just got to *cut that B.S. out!!*

It's thoroughly *not* useful. The only thing worse than slacking off in your practice is feeling like crap for slacking off in your practice. So please don't do that.

Sit with others.

Meditation is most often a solitary pursuit, a time for you to simply be with yourself. However, if it becomes unrelentingly solitary, you may start to feel a bit lost in space or even kind of lonely. While the ability to rest in both spaciousness and solitude are actually quite important, instituting some simple checks and balances prevents confusion as your practice develops. (Believe me, it's easy to become confused! Generations of meditators will tell you so.)

A great way to keep your practice real is to sit with others from time to time. If there is a local (trustworthy) meditation center in your area, you're in luck. (See Appendix C: Resources.) However, if there is no such place within a reasonable radius, don't worry—you're still in luck. Invite a few friends to practice with you and establish a sitting group. It can be as small as two or three people or as large as you like. You could get together once a week or once a month and simply sit for a mutually agreed-to time, followed by a conversation about how the practice is going for each of you.

For readers of this book, I've created a "Sit Alone Together" (free) guide with tips and ideas for forming such a group yourself. The guide has a link to a video with guided meditation instruction especially for a small group. You could play it at your first session together to help you get started. Visit this link for the free download: www.susanpiver.com/shn-resources.

Optional

Have a dharma book near your meditation space and read a paragraph, page, or chapter before or after your practice. When we marry even the slightest bit of study to our practice, our realization deepens.

For a list of tools I suggest, such as cushions, timers, and benches, please visit www.susanpiver.com/shn-resources. These are simply tools I suggest. Don't spend too much time trying to establish the perfect rig. When in doubt, practice. Whether you're sitting on a special cushion or the couch, the important thing is to practice.

ELEVEN

• • •

on posture

Your meditation practice begins by taking your seat. This is no small piece of the practice. The details of the posture are very specific. If you begin to read about it, you'll learn about the magical possibilities inherent in taking the meditation posture correctly. Your natural vitality is strengthened. The chakras align. Your heart opens. Liberation is possible. I actually believe all of these things are true; however, I'm not sure what they really mean so I can't say much about them.

What I can tell you is this. The sitting meditation posture supports you to synchronize body and mind. When they are synchronized, you relax. That seems to be how we are built. And when you are relaxed, you are strong, flexible, and present.

In our device-driven, insanely speedy world we need special techniques to bring our mind and body into the same place. Meditation is one such technique. The breath is the bridge that connects body and mind and when you place attention on it, you are strengthening that bridge.

Too, breath only happens in the present. There is no such thing as taking a breath in the past or the future. So when your mind rides the breath, then, it is in the present moment.

With this, as mentioned, we relax. This is not the relaxation of watching TV or playing a game—which is more like spacing out. (I have nothing against spacing out, by the way.) This is the kind of relaxation you feel when you become absorbed in something. You may be working quite hard—on discovering a new mathematical formula, pulling weeds out of the garden, or listening to a friend—but when we are fully engaged, there is also a sense of flow. It is invigorating.

It is so common to take a punishing mental attitude toward our bodies. The truth is, most of us are doubtful about our bodies. It is not beautiful enough. It is not fit enough. It can't digest dairy. It needs too much sleep. It is scarred. When you sit down to meditate, instead of measuring its attributes and defects, you extend the hand of friendship toward your body. We release our body from expectations that it perform for us. We let it off the hook for being some kind of tool that we can manipulate in service of things like perfection, accomplishment, and even love. This in itself has tremendous healing capacity. All you have to do is sit up straight. Your own natural elegance will do the rest.

I often hear from people who would like to change one or more details of the posture. "It is easier for me to focus when I close my eyes." "Instead of resting my hands palms down just above the knee, I make *jnana* mudra because that is what we do in yoga." "I do my meditation lying down."

Now, I don't want to be all Mindfulness Bitch here, but it is important to actually follow the posture instructions quite precisely. The details are there for a reason. I can't tell you what all the reasons are, because I don't know them. Over time, however, you find out what they are. Through applying the technique rather than making advance judgments about what the technique is or should be, the posture begins to work on you rather than the other way around.

Personally, I find the posture to be a source of dignity. I have taken it countless times and each time I do, I feel, not comforted exactly, but empowered. You take your seat right in the middle of your life.

So take note of your impulse to introduce refinements. It may be rooted in great wisdom or you may simply be trying to entertain yourself because you feel sad or bored or nervous. It is so useful to practice staying put, solid as a mountain, completely committed, no matter the winds of emotion or agitation. In this way, your practice becomes an anchor that you can set down anytime, not just when you are meditating.

Of course if you have a physical injury or impediment, that is a different story. Please use common sense. Better yet, sign up for a meditation class and get support and guidance from a teacher.

In my Shambhala lineage, we often speak about "taking your seat," which means to own your particular spot with neither false humbleness nor false pride. You can rouse this each time you sit down to meditate. True humbleness and true pride look the same. They look like genuineness. They look like an invitation. They look exactly like you. When you take your seat in full and unabashed possession of both your wisdom and your confusion, the teaching channel opens in a most interesting way.

Please have a look at the accompanying drawings for illustrations of good and bad ways to sit.

Good posture for sitting on the floor: Knees and pelvis create a supportive triangle. For many people, this is the best posture, or the best one to work toward. (See stick figure 1.) For some, though, floor sitting is too stressful on the hips and groin. In the side view (see stick figure 2), notice the straight line of her neck and relaxed palms.

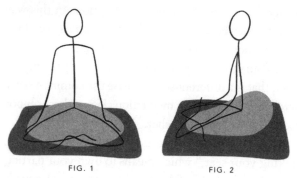

FIG. 1   FIG. 2

Bad posture for sitting on the floor: Don't arch or round your back too much—look at the potential for neck strain in both cases. (See stick figures 3 and 4.)

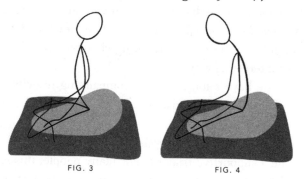

FIG. 3   FIG. 4

Good posture for those who prefer to sit with the knees slightly elevated: Sitting with the knees slightly elevated is fine if you prefer that. (See stick figures 5 and 6.)

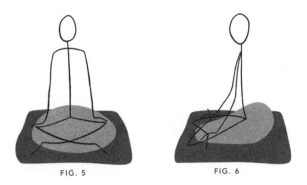

FIG. 5   FIG. 6

Good posture for those who prefer to sit on a meditation bench: Some people prefer to sit on a meditation bench, knees down and in front. This is fine, too. (See stick figures 7 and 8.)

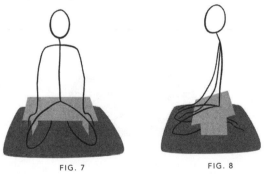

FIG. 7   FIG. 8

Bad posture for those who prefer to sit on a meditation bench: But there's still no need to slump. (See stick figure 9.)

FIG. 9

Ideal posture: Full lotus is the ideal posture for meditating—but not necessary! (See stick figure 10.) Don't try this at home.

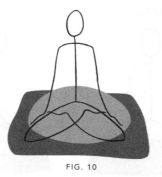

FIG. 10

Sitting on a chair: If you choose to sit on a chair, that is great. Sit with your feet flat on the floor and scoot forward so that your back isn't leaning on anything. (See stick figure 11) If you find any back strain in this position, experiment with placing a cushion underneath your feet to raise your knees to be level with your hips.

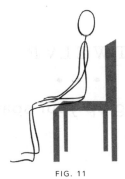

FIG. 11

TWELVE

· · ·

setting up your space

It helps your practice to take root when you establish a place for it. While it does not have to be fancy, it should be tidy and clean.

Something shifts when we walk into a space that has been cared for. We slow down. We feel respectful and respected. We want to spend time there

I remember once, a long time ago, my husband and I went to visit a friend of his mother's. She was in her eighties and somehow had found her way from being a 1950s suburban housewife to being a Zen practitioner. When I met her, she had been practicing for nearly thirty years. For most of that time, she had lived very simply in a tiny rent-controlled apartment on Manhattan's Upper East Side. The moment I stepped into her home, I felt transported into a place of beauty, sanity, and elegance. However, the carpets, sofa, and chairs were threadbare. The knickknacks on her shelves were pedestrian and even a little chipped. Her clothing had clearly been in her possession for decades.

She offered us tea and set out a plate of store-bought cookies. For the life of me, I can't put my finger on what made her home seem like a palace and she its queen. Every single possession shone with the glow of being well-loved and cared about. My cup of tea and cookie tasted delicious. When I sat on her couch, I sat up straight and when she spoke, I listened carefully. Her manner was exceedingly gentle, humble, and quiet. Everything seemed very slowed-down and dignified. It was the most regal place I'd ever visited.

What made it so? Nothing was expensive, fancy, or sophisticated. The glow emanated from her caring heart, care which extended to everything and everyone in that space. It was not just that she kept her things orderly and clean—she actually *cared* for them. Here, caring does not mean fussing to get everything just so. It means placing your loving attention on it. "This is what Zen really is," I remember thinking.

When we extend care to the environment, the environment itself becomes a place of kindness. We can generate such an environment for our meditation space by simply paying attention to it.

The space doesn't have to be large; it can be as small as a corner of your bedroom. But keep that corner clean. Rather than tossing a couch cushion on the floor, cover it with a beautiful fabric or invest in a meditation cushion. If you sit in a chair, choose a nice one. Don't be nutty, but acknowledge and respect your intention in the things you surround yourself with and use. If you like, you could have a small table or stool in front of you as you meditate. On it, you could place any number of things—a candle, flowers, seashells, stones, or a picture of someone or something that inspires you. Again, keep it simple. These small touches of caring will invite you back to your meditation cushion again and again.

THIRTEEN

• • •

keeping it sacred

It happens to all of us at some point that meditation becomes another thing to cross off the to-do list. Something to slog through with the hope that it will *do* something for us. I mean, why spend all this time if you're not going to "get" something? Well, you do get something, that is for sure. But the getting seems to happen when we approach our practice with a sense of freshness, free from any agenda. How do we keep our practice from slipping from sacred to self-improvement? I once asked my own meditation teacher this question, and he said, "Oh, that's simple. Just make offerings, request blessings, and dedicate the merit." That's pretty much all he said, but in the intervening years, I've thought about this pithy instruction quite a bit and have shared it with my own students.

I highly recommend these three steps, as described below, in connection with your spiritual practice—all of which, though they sound religious (offerings? blessings?), actually have nothing to do with beliefs or ethics or rules. If you approach them in a certain way, they are actually very personal and have the capacity to re-situate meditation in the realm of the spiritual rather than the psychological (or religious).

The first two of these steps should be done before you do your spiritual practice:

Make offerings.

When you walk into a shrine room of any religion, there are often flowers, candles, and incense. These are offerings. You can make a similar type of setup in your home, by creating a smaller version of a traditional shrine. Shrine objects tend to center around the senses: things you can see, smell, taste, touch, or hear. Images of respected figures, flowers or scented candles, sweets, beautiful fabrics, and music are often included in sacred spaces. A shrine or altar is a way of focusing the energy of these offerings, so a table covered in brocade holding a candle and a photograph is a very simple way of showcasing your offerings. It's not important to make your altar table the most beautiful in the history of the world. What is important is that it be clean and heart-felt. Or you can simply place some fresh flowers next to a picture of someone or something you love and aspire to emulate. You can light a candle as an offering of warmth, light, and safety. And, when in doubt, the best offering is one you can always make, no matter where you are or how you feel: and that is your own experience in the moment.

So, before meditation, touch in with how it feels to be you right now. Maybe you feel great, crappy, or all of the above. Feel it. Offer it to whomever or whatever you hold sacred by saying something like, "I offer exactly who I am right now to the highest wisdom and goodness I can imagine."

You don't have to know exactly what this means, just rouse a sense of generosity.

Request blessings.

Requesting blessings, as with offerings, requires you to give up knowing what a blessing looks like exactly. Requesting of the gods what you think will make you happy (bring me my dream job) is like making a reservation at a five-star restaurant and then asking if you can go back into the kitchen and cook your own meal. Instead of cooking your own food, just try to order what sounds good to you. *Please let me feel satisfied in my work* is better than *Please make me VP of finance*.

Other options include *Please let me find love. I wish to be free of this pain. Please teach me to forgive.* These are good, basic requests that will allow a master chef to serve you something that exceeds all expectations.

It's totally okay to ask the world to bless you. And who do you ask? If you are a Christian, you could ask Jesus. If you are Buddhist, you can ask for your teacher's blessing. You can seek the blessings of magic if you are an alchemist, of Gandhi if you're a pacifist, of the earth if you're a pagan. The idea is to seek the blessings of your lineage.

What lineage do you belong to? Is it a religious tradition? Maybe so, maybe not. Maybe you're of the lineage of poets or scientists, of painters, mothers, CEOs, crusaders, or lovers.

Get a sense of your heart's lineage and, in whatever way feels natural to you, request the blessings of that line.

Requesting blessings is predicated on the assumption that greater powers are at work. This could mean any number of things to each of us. That greater power could be God, a deity, an angel, or the quality of human goodness. It could also be something unnamable and perhaps this is the most trustworthy power of all. It doesn't really matter what you call this greater power. The only thing that seems required is to not quite understand what it is. Whenever anyone seems to know with too much certainty just what this power is, where it lives, what it thinks, and the primary means of access, I become a bit suspicious. Sure, all sorts of explanations make sense. But the only thing I know is that the moment I think I understand the sacred oneness of existence, I've stepped outside of that oneness and therefore can't be trusted.

So when you request blessings, no matter how certain you are of where and whom they come from, let there also be a little bit of not-knowing.

After these two steps, do your practice. Then, after meditation, do this third step:

Dedicate the merit.

Once you have finished your practice, connect with whatever benefit you may have created for yourself through undertaking this practice. Once you have this felt sense, give it away. In whatever way feels natural for you, make the aspiration that the results of your practice could be used to also benefit others. This is very important. My teacher, Sakyong Mipham, says that not dedicating the merit is like not hitting the "save" button on your Word document before shutting the program down.

FOURTEEN

• • •

obstacles and antidotes

We all have difficulty with committing to the meditation cushion. I totally understand. When you sit on the cushion, you're agreeing to sit down with the unknown. Sometimes this feels terrifying, sometimes exciting, but, mostly, it's just kind of ordinary—and it's this ordinariness that might make us think "nothing is happening" or "I must be doing this wrong." And then we give up. However, it's actually considered a good sign when the practice becomes a bit boring—you've stopped trying to entertain yourself. So hang in there with all the ups and downs and lack of ups and downs.

Buddhists have written a lot on overcoming the obstacles to a meditation practice, because people have been encountering these obstacles for, like, twenty-five hundred years. There are three main obstacles.

Laziness

This is basically the king of all obstacles. It is so complex and prevalent that three separate kinds have been identified:

Regular. No one needs to explain what this kind of laziness is. It's the kind where you lie on the couch and watch television or play Candy Crush instead of getting yourself to the cushion. "Oh just one more game . . . " (Or episode or chapter or cookie.)

Becoming disheartened. According to Buddhist thinking, when you've allowed yourself to become discouraged, this is a sign that you have forgotten about the power and benefits of meditation. "Nothing is happening." "I have better things to do with my time." "I've been at this for __ minutes, days, years, and I still don't get it." When thoughts such as these arise in your mind, you have lost faith in the technique. And let's face it, nothing *is* happening when you meditate. The benefits of meditation don't usually arise during practice— they arise in your life. Sometimes we forget this.

Being too busy. Yes, this sounds a bit counterintuitive. Aren't busy people busy because they're important? Maybe. But when you're too busy to honor your highest priorities—which are understanding the meaning of your life, discovering your wisdom, and offering your heart—that is a sign that you've let something slip due to laziness.

The antidotes are as follows:

Trust. At some point, you had an insight that meditation was valuable. That's what made you decide to try it out. You can trust that insight. Recall it to yourself before you practice.

Aspiration. What arises when you remember what brought you to meditation in the first place? You can trust that insight.

Effort. The truth is, there are no tricks. At a certain point, you just have to get yourself to sit on the cushion and begin. At first, this is difficult. But as the practice takes root in your life, stamina increases and the ability to put in effort is natural.

Pliancy. If you practice for a few minutes every day, this is way better than a lot of minutes on a few days. Routine is the key. Continuity is more important than duration. Then at some point your practice reaches the kind of critical mass that brushing your teeth has. It's just something you do and it feels icky if you don't do it.

Forgetting the instructions

The instructions are not that complicated; how is it that we could forget them? Well, it's not that you forget how to meditate exactly; it's more that you find

you've let certain parts of the technique, even important ones, slip. I can't tell you how many times I've sat
on my cushion for five, ten minutes, before I remember, oh yeah, I'm supposed to be paying attention to
my breath, not thinking about all the things I have to
do today. Or I notice that my hands are gripping my
knees instead of resting on them. Beyond this, you
may forget that the instruction is to let thought go. It
is not at all uncommon to "forget" some small or large
piece of the technique.

The antidote is to refresh your memory. Go over
the technique in your mind before you actually begin
to practice. Read a page or two from a book about
meditation that describes the technique. From time to
time, use a meditation video that guides you through
the practice. I guarantee that as you reflect, read, or
watch, you'll experience at least one moment of "Oh
yeah! I forgot about that bit."

Laxity or elation

It's possible that at some point in your meditation,
you'll fall asleep. Or if not fall asleep, you'll drowse
instead of practice. Or you may apply the technique in
a loosey-goosey kind of way. A general kind of sleepi-
ness (or laxity) descends on your practice.

It is also possible that the opposite may occur from
time to time. Although it's never happened to me, I

know some people who report earth-shattering insights or great shock waves of energy.

While this is lovely, it is also considered a distraction.

The antidote to both is the same: let go and return your attention to the breath.

If you have a fabulous experience or an awful one on the cushion, it's all the same. Don't let either convince you that you're doing it right or wrong. Just keep coming back. As long as you're coming back—to your breath, to your cushion—there is no way you can do it wrong. (However, there is also no way you can do it right. So you can relax.)

I also suggest the following as a way to stay with your practice:

Find community. It is so helpful to practice with others. You can go to a Shambhala center if your town has one, or a Zen center, or a vipassana center. You could join the Open Heart Project. Most meditation centers have public sitting where you can get some instruction or just sit with others. It's enormously supportive and inspiring to be with others who are working with their minds as you endeavor to.

Last, remember that if you take your seat, rouse the intention and aspiration to meditate, and apply the technique wholeheartedly, the practice itself will guide you down the path. All you have to do is walk through the gate.

FIFTEEN

• • •

meditation and depression

Personal disclosure: I have struggled with depression for my entire life, since I was a small child. I really don't know why and I sort of don't really care why anymore—it's apparently just part of who I am. Nonetheless, I have had to find a way to work with it because it has at times been nearly debilitating.

It always begins with a feeling of heaviness in my body, a strong sense of being weighted down, and a kind of mental activity that I know quite well: no matter where I look in my life—to my work, relationships, bank account, home, body, past, and future—it all looks bleak. Very bleak. In times past, I used to dive into stories about how it got to be this way. True stories, I might add. *I missed this opportunity. I made that wrong choice. My abilities are limited.* Yes, true—on one hand. And utterly meaningless on the other. Through my meditation practice, I've learned other ways of relating to depression, not as an onus but as a strange and dark gift.

Typically, there are three suggestions made for liberating ourselves from negativity.

The first school of thought suggests that the negative stories we tell ourselves are basically made up in the first place and we should make up positive ones to replace them. I've tried this. It doesn't work. It is claustrophobic and encourages aggressively wishful thinking.

The next is to find whatever therapy or therapies work for you and get to the bottom of why this is happening in the first place. This can be very wonderful. It provides important insights about causes and triggers; however, it may not make you feel less pain.

The third way is not about converting thoughts from one form to another nor is it about making a case study. Rather, it is a deceptively simple piece of advice given by Chögyam Trungpa, the Tibetan meditation master who transmitted the Shambhala teachings in the West. It was this: "You could always just cheer up."

When I first heard that, I was kind of offended. What do you mean, "just cheer up?" It sounded like what people used to tell me when I was little, some variation of "Why are you always so serious?" or "You're too sensitive. Smile!" Stuff that used to make me really mad. But Trungpa Rinpoche did not mean this. He meant you could always simply let go of what is plaguing you—no matter how heavy and sorrowful—and take a breath of fresh air.

To do so, your meditation practice is very, very helpful.

I've tried it countless times. When I catch myself falling into a pit of despair over loved ones who are suffering from illness, for example, or my finances (also suffering from illness I might add), or my ability to make my dreams manifest—I say to myself as I plummet, "You could always just cheer up," and, amazingly, even if it's only for a moment, *I do*. It has nothing to do with talking myself out of what is bothering me by convincing myself that it will all be okay for this reason or that. It has nothing to do with fake-deleting negative thoughts and fake-inserting ~~wishful thinking~~ positive thoughts and it has nothing to do with causes and conditions. Instead, it has to do with letting it all, all, all go and reconnecting with—well, what would you call it? The present moment. Nowness. Space.

You could try it. It's really simple to get the sense of how. Have you ever been in a fitness class, for example, where they tell you to tense up your shoulders . . . hold . . . hold . . . hold . . . and then release? When you do this, there is a sudden rush of clean energy. You can also do this with your mind. When you feel really depressed—or grief-stricken or angry or disappointed or what have you—you could tune into it. Intensify it. Locate it in your physical or emotional body, or in the environment—and then *intensify, intensify, intensify—LET GO*. Try it. See what happens. What happens for me is there is a sudden rush (even if sometimes it is a tiny one), of life force and renewed energy.

The therapeutic path for working with depression meets depressive patterns as wave forms, which is awesome. In this way, you can work with the ongoing and pervasive presence of negativity. The cheer-up path for working with depression meets such patterns as particles. We can work with each one in the moment it appears. Together, these two approaches, wave and particle, can create quantum change in our relationship to depression.

It all begins with catching yourself, with the ability, no matter how momentary, to know what is happening in your own mind—as if a lightning strike suddenly lit up a dark valley and you see exactly what is going on. Then you can step outside of your heavy, believable, painful, oppressive thought patterns. With this step away, you introduce a moment of possibility . . . of change . . . of a fresh start . . . you *cheer up*. And everything is possible. Your meditation practice teaches this, exactly.

SIXTEEN

• • •

meditation and creativity

The other day, I read a tweet from someone looking for advice about taking up meditation for creative reasons. Could it help one become more creative, they wondered?

I've had ample opportunity to study this question. I lead meditation and writing retreats that are about reconnecting with our own creativity and, beyond that, with the moment of inspiration. And after all, what is creativity, exactly, besides a continuous series of moments of inspiration? Which raises the questions: What is inspiration and where does it come from? Can my meditation practice help?

When it comes to the latter question, the answer is "absolutely" and "maybe not."

Fascinatingly, Dictionary.com offers us this definition of "to inspire": "To infuse into the mind; to communicate to the spirit; to convey, as by a divine or supernatural influence; to disclose preternaturally; to produce in, as by inspiration." And this: "To draw in by the operation of breathing; to inhale."

At no point is the definition offered: "to be clever" or "to impress." Rather, the definition points to something far more simple, receptive, and intimate.

When I think of inspiration, the word that comes to me is "clarity." Suddenly I see something that I hadn't seen before—not because it wasn't there, but because I simply hadn't noticed it before. Inspiration comes not from conquering new horizons of thought or acquiring skills I had been lacking, but from relaxing into a more spacious view. This is why our most interesting inspirations often happen when we do not expect them, while showering, dreaming, or driving. When we stop striving—even to be more creative, relaxed, or intelligent—moments of clear seeing arise.

Our meditation practice teaches this exact skill: to relax our minds by resting attention on breath—without agenda. The moment we apply an agenda to our meditation practice, even a noble one such as practicing in order to be more creative, the energy of the practice is drained. When we are able to let go of conventional agendas, our brilliance is unleashed. This is how creativity works. I don't know why.

One of the greatest teachers ever of the Enneagram (about which I am passionate), the Chilean psychiatrist and brilliant thinker Claudio Naranjo, said about music, "Only repetition invites spontaneous innovation," and of course this is true of all the arts. You can't sit down at your computer or pick up your guitar or paintbrush and command yourself to innovate. Much sloppiness results from such an approach unless you just happen to get lucky. But we can do better than hoping to get lucky in art, by learning to work with our minds skillfully and openly. Meditation is a very powerful way to do so—but only if it is practiced free from any and all agendas. At this point, one's vision expands. The repetition of focusing on breath—breath—breath also, somehow connects you to a much larger space. Zooming in, we pan out.

Creativity is predicated on just this form. Take writing, for example. If the focus of meditation is breath, the focal point of writing is a word. No matter how hard you try, you can write only one word at a time. Word—word—word. Even if it happens very fast, each one is still selected. At the same time, how do you know what to say? I have no idea, by the way. All I notice is that the "what to say" seems to arise from space and this is what creates good writing (or music or dance, and so on). If you sit down to write already knowing exactly what to say, you will end up with a textbook or a report. If you allow the writing to arise in the act of writing, it seems to result in something fresh. So both meditation and creativity share this: each is *simultaneously* one-pointed and panoramic. As I have practiced both over the years, I have come to see that there is actually no difference in technique, none whatsoever.

I once attended a small gathering to hear a talk on creativity by the late classical music composer and devoted Buddhist practitioner Peter Lieberson. Someone asked him about his daily routine. Did he work on one piece continuously? Did he work particular hours? How did he know what to create? All he said in answer was this, "The most important moment in my process is the moment before I begin," and I have ruminated on this countless times. I think what he meant was to release all agendas, ideas, expectations, hopes, and fears, which are always obstacles. Upon such release, rather than encountering an abyss, one is reconnected with the great and luminous field that is inspiration itself.

So, can meditation help you become more creative? Definitely. And no way.

SEVENTEEN

• • •

meditation and compassion

To be a spiritual warrior, one must have a broken
heart; without a broken heart and the sense of tenderness and vulnerability that is in one's self and
all others, your warriorship is untrustworthy.

— *Chögyam Trungpa*

If the practice of Buddhist meditation is associated with
anything, it is with the generation and expression of
compassion. One of the central tenets of the dharma
is compassion in all its forms, relative and absolute. In
many ways, the entire point of all the practice and study
we do is to become more compassionate. This compassion is meant for all beings, no matter what: the people you love, the people you like, the people you don't
know, and the people you hate. All of them are worthy

of your compassion, and in each case, we are to find a way to express it.

The Buddhadharma is not, however, associated with the practice of being a candy-ass. In fact, compassion is among the fiercest, bravest, and most uncompromising states of being that you can ever imagine. It is really easy to become confused about this and imagine that it means being sweet and nice all the time. It does not. Chögyam Trungpa famously coined the phrase "idiot compassion," which is an interesting thing for a Buddhist teacher to say. If it is always appropriate to express compassion, what then could "idiot compassion" be?

When you think of the word "compassion," what comes to mind? Maybe you get an image of Mother Teresa or a parent holding an infant. Maybe you think of a room full of people who are upset while the compassionate person calms everyone down, or someone who stops at the site of a roadside accident to see if there is anything he can do to help.

You probably don't think of someone who is yelling, walking out, coldly observing the scene around herself, or even brandishing a weapon: however, these too can be gestures of compassion.

Compassion is an inner stance, not an external pose. We can only know the difference with an ongoing connection to our own heart. When we allow ourselves to feel, it is possible to detect what is most compassionate in any situation. When we are afraid to feel, it is not.

So one could say that when we lean into our heart of hearts, we discover the fount of kindness. When we clamp down on our inner experience or avoid emotions, the path to kindness is also obscured. Kindness toward others, then, is actually synonymous with kindness toward self.

This may seem counterintuitive. Many definitions of compassion include putting others before self. This is great, a perfectly sound definition. However, if we think of others *instead* of ourselves, we lose the heart connection that gives rise to compassion altogether. (Pema Chödrön says idiot compassion is "what's called enabling.")

So the compassion formula could look something like this:

1. Encounter event: child crying, fender bender, stupid political warfare (redundant, I know).
2. Notice what you feel and, beyond noticing it, feel it. Would you call it fear, anger, sadness? Find it in your body. Does it feel hot or cold; does it make your shoulders tense or your stomach clench?
3. Relax. (Here, relax means "allow" rather than "tune out.")
4. Let your heart soften to what you feel and allow yourself to fill with it.
5. Reencounter the event and let your heart soften

to those involved, even if only for a moment, and trust whatever instinct arises about what is most helpful. Perhaps it is a hug. Or a phone call for help. Or an angry confrontation with the forces of wrong.

Unless you feel your own heart, you won't know which gesture is kindest. Idiot compassion skips this step.

The source of true compassion is your own heart, and the guiding question is "What is needed in this exact moment?" The source of idiot compassion is concept, and the guiding question is "What do I need to do to feel good about myself?"

I'm not saying this is easy. Compassion consists of two qualities to be held simultaneously. Both are critical. One of them is frightening. It is called "pain." The world is riddled with pain. It is everywhere we look. When we open to the pain in our own hearts, the pain of others also enters, and this can feel quite daunting. However, it is necessary.

The second component is called "love" and refers to the response that naturally arises when we do open to this pain. This is just how we are built. On the heels of pain comes the counterbalance that restores to us the only lasting source of joy.

Someone once said to me that compassion is the ability to hold pain and love in your heart simultaneously, and I have never heard a better, more intimate definition.

As you sit in meditation, the seeds of just such compassion are sown on the wind of breath. With each inhalation, you open to the world, take something in, connect with your life, plant a seed. With each exhalation, you let go and there is something in the letting go that provides the moisture and warmth necessary for the seed to blossom.

Thus compassion takes tremendous courage. It is an act of fearlessness.

You can totally do it. All you have to do is allow your heart to break to the sorrow and beauty of this world.

EIGHTEEN

• • •

meditation and love

When you practice Buddhism, part of the commitment is to take off the training wheels and do your best to put the dharma into play in all situations. It's no longer theoretical. It is your life. It's a fun, scary, and noble challenge—especially when it comes to relationships. How is it possible to apply this ancient wisdom to the reality of falling in love, losing love, surviving without love, and making a relationship last (without losing your soul)?

It is always good to begin at the beginning, which, when it comes to the dharma, means contemplating the four noble truths. When the Buddha became enlightened, people asked him to reveal the truths he had learned. He mentioned four things.

1. Life is suffering. (Doesn't mean "life sucks," by the way. More like, "life changes.")
2. Suffering is caused by attachment. (Pain comes from wanting things to be other than they are.)
3. It is possible to stop suffering. (Phew.)
4. There is an eightfold path to liberate yourself from suffering, which includes such things as Right Speech, Right Action, and so on.

Countless words have been written on each of these four, and you could definitely spend a lifetime in contemplation of just one of them. To apply them to everyday life means to accept that things won't ever quite work out (at least not in any conventional sense); that when you hold on to anything too tightly (even the idea of not holding on to anything too tightly), it backfires; you can definitely figure all this out; and, finally, that there is a step-by-step explanation for how to do so, via practices, insights, devotion, and so on.

Okay, why not! This should work! I can apply these truths to my work—check. My money—check. Family—check. Social concerns—check. The reality of death—check. Romantic relationships—um, wait.

When it comes to love and partnership, I definitely try to wiggle out of the four noble truths. I can halfway toy with accepting that everything changes, even that I will die and this body will be a corpse. But when it comes to love—I need that to be permanent. When my husband tells me he loves me, that cannot change or I'm going to be very, very upset. When we make a commitment to share our lives with each other, that too must be rock solid. And when it comes to acknowledging that, one way or another, this relationship will definitely end, well, I just need that not to be true. Otherwise it is simply unbearable.

(I believe that this, by the way, is why most relationships fail, because to come to terms with this last truth is just too painful. It's easier to break up with someone because they don't make you laugh/take you seriously/earn enough money/eat dairy, but really I think it's because, at some point, we become unbearably precious to each other. But I digress.)

Even among deeply practiced and skillful Buddhists, I can't help but notice that it is difficult to apply the dharma to anything that involves love and sex. When it comes to relationships, we believe our version of reality is absolutely solid and correct. There is no oxygen when you feel neglected, dismissed, suffocated, or enraged by the one you love. Oddly, it is our intimate relationships that most challenge our ability to be open, nonjudgmental, compassionate, and kind.

The hardest people to love are the ones you, well, really love. What is up with that?

This is something I think about all the time. I took the liberty of recasting the four noble truths as they could apply to love.

1. Relationships are uncomfortable.

Right? Whether you're on a blind date, worrying if you'll like each other, or have been married for twenty years—groaning yet again, "Why are you doing that thing that I've asked you eleventy billion times not to do?"—there is a kind of discomfort. Of course, there are also times of sheer delight and deeply gratifying intimacy, but even in the sweet moments, there is the shock (and discomfort) of dissolution.

I've come to think that the most deeply loving gesture I can make within my relationship is to tolerate my own discomfort—to recognize my feelings and leave the story behind; to cease and desist threatening my husband with consequences should he fail to be the person I need him to be rather than the person he is. There are only so many times you can choose your make-believe husband over your real one before something goes bust.

Too, there is something magical, yes magical, about this discomfort. You're right there, never quite in your comfort zone. Always a tiny bit on the edge, like you're trying something new for the very first time. Which, when it comes to love, is not such a bad approach. Brilliance and inspiration and everything fresh is discovered on this edge, including how to open your heart beyond what you ever thought possible.

Of course, your meditation practice teaches you exactly how to ride the waves of delight and discomfort, passion and distance, love and boredom.

2. Thinking that relationships should be comfortable is what makes them uncomfortable.

It is pretty hard to get away from the idea that love is supposed to make you happy. No, wait, it *is* supposed to make you happy—if "happy" means alive, open, giving, and touchable. When it's defined as safe and predictable, getting what you want, or finding the perfect man/woman, we might run into a few problems.

When we say we're looking for love, most of us really mean we're looking for safety, a way to get comfortable. We're looking for someone to love us first, and then we will love them back. (It seems that 99.9 percent of relationship self-help books are about how to get love, not how to give it. That's kind of odd, no?!) "Relationship" is equated with a protective cocoon.

It's understandable. Loving is so vulnerable, maybe the most vulnerable thing you can do. Love is not for sissies. However, there is nothing less safe than love. Love means opening again and again to your beloved, yourself, and your world, and seeing what happens next. The moment you try to make it safe, it ceases to be love. Believe me, I'm not saying you shouldn't be very smart, practical, and skillful when it comes to choosing your relationships. But if you think a relationship is going to protect you from the trials and tribulations of being human, well, that is simply not going to happen.

Luckily, your meditation practice teaches you how to sit with discomfort and, instead of being distracted by it, to notice it, let go, and return to your breath. In love, this applies beautifully, with one key difference. You notice it. Let it go. And return your attention to *your partner*. In this way, your partner becomes the object of your meditation rather than your breath and this is what helps you to stay. And, when it comes to relationships, the capacity to stay is perhaps the most important one of all. (Barring abuse of any kind, of course.)

3. It is absolutely possible to love and be loved unconditionally.

You know this is true. You know it from experience. You are in the house of unconditional love every time you are touched beyond thought by the beauty of your fellow human beings, and every time one is touched by you. Even something as simple as the smile a stranger gives you when you hold the door for him or her qualifies. Or when you are moved by the success of someone you love and feel it as your own. When you are touched by someone's sadness and want to help.

When you open your eyes, you see that such moments are taking place all the time. These agenda-less instances of opening to another are unconditional love. I mean, they are unconditional, right? You're not putting any conditions on things when you simply feel them spontaneously. I rest my case.

This ability to reopen your heart is always possible. Meditation practice teaches us how to not be afraid of what we feel and, further, to actually lean into our hearts, allow them to be touched. When we do so, all we find is tenderness. Don't take my word for this. See for yourself.

4. There is a path that teaches you how and it really works.

You can practice becoming comfortable with discomfort. The sitting practice of meditation teaches you how, exactly, directly, perfectly.

You can practice letting your dear ones—and yourself—off the hook for not being perfect. The practice (and experience) of loving kindness teaches you how.

And you can practice letting life in, allowing people, circumstance, your own brilliance, and your own foibles to touch you deeply. When you know how to navigate from discomfort back to equilibrium through the practice of meditation and can extend yourself to others fearlessly by acknowledging your innate loving kindness, you can stop looking for love. You have made your life into love itself.

Now that we have thought about what meditation is and is not, sorted through the various kinds, and taken a brief look at how it could impact certain aspects of your life, let's keep the exploration going. The seven-day meditation challenge and weekend retreat program described on the coming pages can help you get started.

NINETEEN

• • •

aspire: the seven-day
meditation challenge

If you are ready to bring meditation into your life, I am so glad! Below is a seven-day program for easing your way in. I chose to make this program seven days long so you could get a sense of what it would be like to add meditation into each day of the week. Though I know there is no such thing as "typical," choose a week that accurately reflects a normal seven-day period. If you get to the end and want to keep going, simply repeat for fourteen or twenty-one days or however long it takes you to feel that you are establishing a good groove. And, of course, you are free to revisit this seven-day guided experience whenever you like.

Please visit www.susanpiver.com/shn-resources to find meditation videos created especially for this seven-day program, as well as some additional material that reviews key components of establishing a lasting practice.

Begin by choosing which day of the week you will start this program. Depending on your schedule, it may be best to begin on a Saturday when you have more flexibility, but it is up to you. However, note that the final meditation session is a full thirty minutes long. You may have more time for this lengthier session if you end on a weekend.

A day or two before you're ready to begin, set up your space. It does not have to be fancy in any way and you don't need any special equipment. It does not have to be isolated from the rest of your space and it doesn't even have to be particularly quiet. A nice, clean corner of your room or an easy chair in your living room will do. If you want to use a meditation cushion, that is great, although a chair is also fine. If you do want to use a meditation cushion, it seems to work best to use one that is specifically meant for that purpose. (I've tried to sit on couch cushions or stacks of bed pillows but they always end up feeling uncomfortable.) Rather than plopping down anywhere, the main point is to establish a sense of place for your practice.

In addition to meditation, this program involves keeping a simple practice journal. You can jot down your thoughts on notebook paper, in a diary, or on your smartphone.

The only other thing to do is decide what time you will practice. For most people mornings work best, although you may be a night owl or simply have a lot to do in the mornings. After work or before bed may be the best time for you. If you choose mornings, just get up a few minutes earlier. If you choose evenings, don't wait until you're exhausted and all you want to do is fall into bed. Instead, make your practice a part of your nighttime routine. If you brush your teeth and wash your face before bed, change your routine to brush your teeth, wash your face, and practice meditation. There is nothing magical about this order, and you are free to switch it around. The point is to establish your practice as a habit, and joining it to other habits seems helpful.

Now that you have prepared the space and settled on a day and time, you are ready to begin the program.

Day one

Plan to sit for ten minutes. (Remember, you may use the videos on my site to guide you.) Ten minutes is actually great. If you have trouble completing this, don't worry about it. Tomorrow may be worse! Or better! You never know. In any case, simply completing the allocated period is wonderful. However, if ten minutes seem to go by in a flash and you wish to sit longer, *don't*. Stay with the plan. Develop trust in yourself that you are able to stick with this (or any) program.

At the end of your session, open your practice journal and jot down a few observations about how it went. Keep it simple. Note the time practiced (in this case, ten minutes) and a few words about how it felt: that is, great, awful, boring, confusing, relaxing, and so on. If you have any questions, jot them down too.

Day two

Sit for ten minutes again. At the end, note elapsed time and a few key words indicating the qualities of your practice today. If any insights into yesterday's questions arose, note them. If additional questions arose, note them too. Add any reflections you like.

Day three

Sit for fifteen minutes. Use the meditation video on my site if you'd like. Note elapsed time again and a few key words indicating the qualities of your practice today.

Day four

Sit for fifteen minutes. Today, begin your practice by saying to yourself, "Now is my time to meditate. Everything else can wait." See what it feels like to begin in this way, definitely, surely, with a sense of command. Afterward, make notes again about this particular session.

Day five

Same as day four. P.S., congratulations! You've almost completed your first full week. You may continue to use the video or experiment with sitting on your own, no video. If you choose to do so, you'll need a timer of some sort. You can use an egg timer, an alarm clock, or an app on your smartphone.

Day six

Sit for twenty minutes using the video I created (or not, if you prefer). Make note afterward of how it felt, just as you have in the previous days. Include questions, observations, and thoughts about continuing your practice beyond this seven-day period.

Day seven

Sit for thirty minutes! You can do it! Use my video for support. After your sit, note, again, any qualities you noticed or questions you have.

I congratulate you from the bottom of my heart! It is no small thing to complete seven concurrent days of meditation. Going forward, you now have meditation videos to choose from to guide you in your daily practice. You are also now capable of sitting on your own, without guidance. I suggest that you make your own plan for the next seven days, choosing from these options. Preparing in this way by scheduling your practice into your day can help solidify your commitment to it.

If you would like, please continue the post-meditation journaling practice, making special note of questions. You can search my site (www.susanpiver.com) for answers, e-mail your questions to me (it will take me time to respond, but I will), or look for relevant books or articles.

TWENTY

• • •

to deepen: a weekend meditation retreat at home

When is the best time to take a couple of days out of your routine to reconnect with your heart and soul, your creative muse, your deepest longings—or simply to rest? When is the best time to remember the person who lives and breathes underneath all of your responsibilities, concerns, hopes, and fears?

The best time is now.

This program invites you to go into your room or home, shut the door literally and metaphorically, unplug all connections, and let go of everyday concerns. During this weekend retreat, I ask you to separate yourself from your daily life and immerse yourself in reflective practices. It begins on a Friday at dinnertime and ends on Sunday after lunch.

This program is based on retreats I have led around the world. It is meant to help you go within, rest your mind, and make space for your innate wisdom to arise.

To prepare

1. Select a weekend (or any two-and-a-half-day period) and put it on your calendar. You can start tomorrow or in six months; it doesn't matter. What matters is committing to it. This commitment marks the beginning of the retreat.

2. Set up a meditation area in your home or room. If you already have one, that's great. If not, choose a spot with room for a meditation cushion or a chair.

3. If you feel so moved, create an altar. There is more detail on this earlier in the book, in the section called "Make Offerings" (see chapter 12, "Setting Up Your Space").

4. If you don't have a journal, buy, find, or make one. It can be a beautiful notebook or just some notepaper in a binder. You will be doing a journaling exercise or two during the retreat, so choose paper and a pen you enjoy writing with. Best not to use a computer.

5. Find something to use as a meditation timer. A simple kitchen egg timer will do, or a timer app for your handheld device. But since you will not be going online during the retreat, if you use an app, be sure

to avoid the temptation to check email or revise your Netflix queue.

6. Let those closest to you know you'll be engaged in this program for a weekend. Ask for their understanding and support. Tell them you may not be able to respond to phone calls, texts, or e-mails immediately.

As much as possible, prepare things in advance and lean on family, friends, or roommates to handle your usual daily chores.

7. Get all your grocery shopping done for the weekend before it begins.

8. Choose and purchase a book you'd like to read during the retreat. It is best to choose something that supports you on your inner journey. Use your judgment and select something that will challenge you to delve within rather than escape.

Retreat tools

Meditation
The meditation practice we will be doing is called shamatha. *Shamatha* is a Sanksrit word that means the "practice of tranquillity." So this retreat is an excellent place to begin.

If you have a regular meditation practice, you will simply be doing that technique, but for longer sessions than you may be used to.

If you are new to meditation or if you simply need a refresher, please review the basic instruction here.

Journaling

During your retreat, I ask you to do a very simple journaling exercise following your morning meditation on Saturday and Sunday. It is called "free writing" or "morning pages," as coined by the wonderful writer Julia Cameron. Free writing is simply this: you pick up pen and paper (don't use a computer) and just start writing down whatever comes to mind until you fill three pages. It can be anything. Whatever words are in your head, transcribe them onto the page.

They do not have to make any sense.

They do not have to be punctuated correctly.

Don't worry about spelling.

You never have to read or share these pages.

Usually, free writing pages look something like this:

I don't know why I'm doing this, this makes no sense. My neck hurts. I wonder if that will interfere with my meditation practice. God, I am so worried that so-and-so will email me during this retreat and they'll be pissed if I don't get back right away. I ate too much oatmeal for breakfast. I am so sad that dad is so sick. I wish I could do anything to relieve his suffering.

If only I was a nurse. I should have gone to nursing school!!

Etcetera, etcetera.

The basic rule of thumb is simply to keep your hand moving across the page. You don't have to be a speed demon, but do keep moving. Remember: your thoughts don't have to make sense or be in any discernible sequence. You can even throw these pages away after you're done, if you like.

Depending on how quickly you write, this exercise will take from twenty-five to forty-five minutes.

Nourishment and Health

I'd like to take a moment and visit this important topic.

I suggest a dietary component for the retreat, although not a complicated one: you don't have to give up meat, coffee, or sugar or eat only vegetables, but please simplify the foods you eat during the retreat and, if you can, for a few days in advance of the retreat start date, so you don't have to spend a lot of time during the retreat figuring out a new food-preparation routine.

For the duration of the retreat, the only guideline I suggest is to eat and drink high-quality foods and beverages. This means nothing packaged, processed, or genetically engineered. If you drink coffee, buy organic beans. If you want to eat candy, get some good-quality, minimally processed chocolate. If you eat a ham sandwich for lunch every day, make it nitrate-free and on whole grain bread. Instead of sugared cereals for breakfast, try a granola that isn't too sweet. If you eat meat, buy organic and if you like a glass of wine with dinner, buy yourself a special bottle.

Plan a trip to the health food store or do the best you can at your regular grocery store. For beverages, stick mostly with water, milk (whole, soy, almond, etc.), coffee, tea, and fruit or vegetable juices. Avoid soda unless you'll spend the whole weekend with a headache if you don't get your cola. If you hate to cook and eat only takeout, buy your to-go food from a health-conscious establishment. This is not a diet by any means, and you don't have to get overly strict with yourself; simply try to cut as many chemicals as you can from what you are eating. Doing so will leave your mind clearer.

If you already consume largely unprocessed and organic foods, great. Just keep doing what you are doing. In all cases, try not to use this time to make sweeping changes. Simply avoid bad foods, consume good ones, and keep it very simple.

Also during this time, please avoid excessive alcohol or recreational drugs, because these substances can make meditation very confusing. If you have an alcohol or drug problem or are undergoing medical or psychiatric treatment, please don't start this program. Consult your doctor and wait for a time when you are able to devote your attention to it fully. If you are taking prescription medications, of course you should continue to take them according to your doctor's instructions.

If you have any concern whatsoever about this program, please check with a health professional before beginning it.

Keep It Sacred

To begin this program, please refer back to chapter 13 and review the steps listed in "Keeping It Sacred." Thoroughly refresh your memory about what it takes to create a sanctified endeavor (rather than one rooted in self-improvement).

Rest

It can seem odd to consider rest as a tool, but it is likely to be the most powerful one of the weekend.

We are all so busy.

We are all so preoccupied.

We are all so accustomed to 24/7 entertainment.

Leaving it all behind for an entire weekend can be thrilling, daunting, nerve-wracking, or a delight. During your retreat, it is likely to be all of the above.

This weekend, there will be long periods of time designated for "rest." This can mean any number of things. When it is time to rest, please choose from the following activities only:

Napping

Daydreaming

Reading (something related to your inner pursuits)

Taking a walk

Staring into space

Drawing, painting, photography, writing poetry—any of the arts—but purely for purposes of creative joy. No work!! No trying to prove anything!

Some things notably missing from this list:

Watching TV

Going online

Talking on the phone

Household chores

Errands

Please try to reserve this weekend for the pleasures of rest and solitude.

Rest is different than spacing out. True rest imparts the qualities of absorption and delight. Spacing out tends to make us both dull and speedy.

The schedule

The aforementioned Julia Cameron once said, "The first rule of magic is containment," and I have never heard truer words. Often we think that the way to begin a new program—whether it's a dietary change, a workout routine, or a spiritual practice—is to talk to some friends, read a few books, maybe take a class, and then give it a shot. But there is an additional element that is important to your success: the form you create to stabilize your efforts. Without the proper environment, the excitement and energy of a new endeavor can dissipate rather quickly.

The schedule outlined herein creates the environment. It is the container for this program. It will create the form and structure that will allow the energy to build. Without this containment, there is no energy or magic. So following the program as carefully as you can is important.

The schedule

Now you are ready to practice.

Once you have finished your practice, connect with

whatever benefit you may have created for yourself through undertaking this practice. Once you have this felt sense, give it away. In whatever way feels natural for you, make the aspiration that the results of your practice could be used to also benefit others. This is very important. As mentioned in chapter 13, my teacher, Sakyong Mipham, says that not dedicating the merit is like not hitting the "save" button on your Word doc before shutting the program down.

If you belong to a tradition that employs a traditional dedication of merit (mine is on the last page of this book), you could use that. It's also great to simply say to yourself, "I offer my practice so that it may benefit everyone." Give it away.

Friday

When you come home from work Friday night, make sure your meditation area is set up. Sometime in the evening, have a seat on your meditation cushion with your journal for a brief journaling exercise. Settle onto your cushion and take a moment to just sit there and appreciate wherever you are. What can you see, hear, smell, and so on?

Noticing the space you're in is a simple way to come into the present moment.

Open your journal and finish these sentences:

Please help me to _____ so that I may _____.

Please guide me to _____ so that I may _____.

Please show me _____ so that I may _____.

Please teach me _____ so that I may _____.

Let these sentiments be your offering for tonight.
Practice meditation for ten minutes before bed.
Dedicate the merit.

Saturday
(Times are approximate. I've started your day at 7 AM,
but if that makes you nuts, shift everything an hour
back or forward to accommodate your body rhythms.)

7:00–7:30 *Meditation.* If you're accustomed to ten-
minute sits, this could seem like a lot. That's okay. Go
for it. Use your timer, commit, and see what happens.
It may be way easier or harder than you thought, or it
may be none of the above.

7:30–8:15 *Free Writing.* Get out your journal and simply let the words flow.

8:15–9:45 *Breakfast Prep, Consumption, Clean Up.* Prepare yourself a delicious breakfast, based on what "delicious" means to you. If you're an "eggs and bacon"
gal, go for it. If you're a "just a cup of coffee" guy, go
for it. Whatever you choose, make your food of the

highest quality possible, to the best of your ability to find and afford it. Feed yourself well, not according to the latest health findings nor as an act of indulgence. Feeding yourself well means putting good-quality ingredients down the hatch. Nothing processed. No chemicals.

Make sure to clean up—not OCD-style, but thoroughly. There is something delightful about finishing the job wholeheartedly. And right now, you've got nothing but time . . .

9:45–11:30 *Rest*. As you may recall, your choices for rest include sleeping, daydreaming, reading something uplifting, going for a walk, just staring into space, and so on. Nothing to accomplish. Nothing to prove.

11:30–12:00 *Meditation*. Let yourself enjoy another period of breath-awareness meditation. Notice how (or if) this session differed from the morning practice. If you feel like journaling about your experience, please do.

If you feel like writing a poem, please do. If you do not, please don't.

12:00–2:00 *Lunch Prep, Consumption, Clean Up*. Make yourself an awesome lunch. Best to keep it kind of light, otherwise your afternoon practice could be on the sleepy side. As you are preparing your food, just prepare your food. Don't listen to music or flip through a magazine. Just prepare, eat, and clean up. Take your time.

2:00–5:00 *Rest*. At this point, you may be growing weary of rest. Seriously. Hang in there with it. Don't give in to the temptation to just quickly check email or catch thirty minutes of *Real Housewives of Orange County*. It would be great if you could fit taking a walk into this time period. I highly recommend choosing a dharma book to accompany you during your retreat. Reading about meditation is especially helpful. For suggested books, see Appendix C: Resources.

5:00–5:30 *Meditation*.

5:30–7:00 *Dinner Prep, Consumption, Clean Up*.

7:00–8:00 *Journaling Exercise (Optional)*. Retreat is a great time to step back and take a larger than usual view of your life. The purpose of this exercise isn't to get you to see what needs changing or how you can improve things—it's simply meant to help you contemplate your situation within a peaceful environment.

1. What three things do I love about myself?
2. What three things scare me about myself?
3. How can I honor my body?

4. What can't I say?
5. What can't I feel?
6. Who do I need to forgive?
7. Who needs to forgive me?
8. What is unfolding in my life right now?
9. Who are my true friends?
10. What is my intuition about what is unfolding in my life?

Take your time answering these questions. Let each one act as a writing prompt and just start putting words on the page in response. See what happens. You can answer all of them or pick and choose the ones that appeal to you most.

8:00–8:30 *Meditation*. This is your final practice session of the day. Please give yourself props for spending two whole hours in meditation practice on this day. That is such an awesome achievement.

8:30 *Dedicate the Merit*. Hang out until bedtime. It's totally fine to go to bed as early as possible. Let yourself enjoy the luxury of s l e e p.

Sunday
The Sunday schedule is largely a reprise of Saturday morning. Your retreat will end at lunch.

You are obviously free to resume your regular activities when the retreat is over, but, if possible, try to keep the rest of the day simple.

7:00–7:30 *Meditation*

7:30–8:15 *Free writing*

8:15–9:45 *Breakfast prep, consumption, clean up*

9:45–11:30 *Rest*

11:30–12:00 *Meditation*

12:00–2:00 *Lunch prep, consumption, clean up*

2:00 *Dedicate the merit*

The best way to end a meditation retreat is to end it when it's over. Meaning, don't end it before it's over (oh, well, there's only an hour left, I might as well stop now) and don't prolong it beyond the end by trying to hang on to a peaceful vibe.

Just as you stay with the entire out-breath during meditation practice, not abandoning it to skip ahead to the next in-breath, don't abandon your retreat. Stay, stay, stay with it until the end. But no further.

Don't hang on to it or push it away. Simply watch it dissolve. This itself is excellent practice.

As your weekend draws to a close, please accept my gratitude and appreciation for your having completed it. This is no small thing. If you'd like to share what it was like for you, I know that I and the entire Open Heart Project community would love to hear about it. You can subscribe to the Open Heart Project newsletter by visiting my website and it is also a great way to receive ongoing (free) meditation instruction from me.

EPILOGUE

• • •

personal story

I have been practicing meditation for close to twenty years. It may sound clichéd, but I truly can't imagine who I would be without this practice. It has helped me build a life of joy and meaning and given me ways to cope when joy and meaning seem to disappear. I am so lucky to have encountered this practice which, given the circumstances under which I grew up, was unlikely to begin with.

I grew up in the 1970s in the suburbs of a large metropolitan city, and if you did too, you will need no explanation of how bland, sterile, and conventional the atmosphere was. From jump street, I did not feel at home. While I was born into enviable external circumstances (stable home life, enough food and money, good education), the internal circumstances were another matter. My earliest memories were of being, well, terrified. There really is no other word for it. I was plagued by night fears and nightmares. I was afraid of the dark, sleep, intruders, ghosts, burglars, murderers. I suffered from insomnia. This was all before the age of ten. I have no idea why and maybe there is no "why." (Perhaps you too are one of those people who was born with a jumpy nervous system and a deep sense of unease.) I believe that I was perpetually close to a nervous breakdown from the ages of about ten to fifteen. It was not pretty. By my early teens, in addition to being fearful, I was cranky, argumentative, and really angry. Perhaps unsurprisingly, those around me were too.

For some unknown reason, my coping method was to reject everything anyone told me and refuse to meet anyone's expectations. No one could tell me what to do, no one. For example, it was assumed that I would be bat mitzvahed as had every other child in my family. No, I said, no way. I don't believe in God and I won't be a hypocrite. You can forget it. A few years later, I reported to everyone that actually I did believe in God, just not their God and I had converted myself to Christianity.

You want me to learn to play an instrument? I refuse to practice. You want me to meet your friends? I'm going to hide in my room. You say education is important and all my peers are planning to become doctors and lawyers? Well, my plan is to flunk eighth grade, barely graduate high school, refuse college, and become a cocktail waitress.

Whatever I was expected to do, I rejected. My parents were on edge. My teachers did not know how to teach me. Nothing in my surroundings made me feel grounded or seen—and rather than trying to fit in to alleviate this anxiety, I embraced not fitting in as my preferred path. I had no idea who I was. I just knew I wasn't who everyone was telling me I should be, but I had no leads on any alternatives. I became very depressed. I felt very alone. I felt crazy.

I brought this fear, restlessness, and disorientation into my early twenties. I worked as a cashier, waitress, and taxi driver and lived for some years perilously close to broke. One day, I was sitting in my cab on a hot summer night when a song came on the radio that said, "There's something happening somewhere, baby, I just know that there is." For some unknown reason, that woke me up. It all happened in a nanosecond. The next day, I threw my stuff in the back of my (sister's) car and drove the f*&k away. I didn't know where I was going and I didn't know what I was going to do when I got there; all I knew was I was headed for "somewhere". (Thank you, Boss.)

Luckily for me, "somewhere" turned out to be Austin, Texas, because my car broke down there and I didn't have enough money to get it fixed. Well, I thought, I guess I live in Austin, Texas, now. In this precise moment, on that very day, my life began to turn around. I got a great, great job. Yes, I was still a waitress, but I was a cocktail waitress in the coolest nightclub on earth with live music seven days a week. *Incredible, mind-blowing music.* My world became all about the blues. I got to hear (and serve drinks to and witness late-night card games with and hear backstage chatter from) Albert King, Albert Collins, Memphis Slim, Matt Murphy, Buddy Guy, Junior Wells, Clifton Chenier, John Lee Hooker, Bobby "Blue" Bland, Lazy Lester, Jimmy Rogers, Eddie Taylor—the list goes on and on. Every once in a while people would drop by to sit in. By "people" I mean Stevie Ray Vaughan. Jimmie Vaughan. Bono. Bruce Willis. (??!) (I could tell you stories, oh, I could tell you stories, but that would be a whole different book.) These superstars were backed by the most soulful house band you could ever imagine. One of the guitar players was my boyfriend!!! After the gig, we'd go for breakfast, then home to sleep until noon, get up, listen to music, go to work, and listen some more. It was pretty much heaven. It was authentic, soulful, and real, the very qualities most notably missing from the world I grew up in. I found myself in a place of character and depth, rooted in its own lineage, the very opposite of a suburb. I began to soften. A lot. After a very tomboyish life, and a semireckless life, I started to feel like (and act like and dress like) a woman.

I let down my guard.

I fell in love.

After only a few months of this completely wonderful experience, I was in a truly brutal car wreck. I was driving home one night, minding my own business (in a sweet restored '67 Beetle), when a drunk driver ran a red light (in a Buick) and T-boned the bejesus out of me. Out the passenger door I went, twenty yards down the road, basically crushed. (Or so I hear. I have no memory of any of it.) I ended up in the hospital for several months and then it took a good few years before I began to feel like myself again. Rather than a reason to close back up, this experience caused me to soften even further, because I found that in my new life I was surrounded by love.

At some point during this period, I went to a yoga retreat center. I had never done yoga before. This was the eighties and yoga centers were still considered kooky. But my brother (who was and remains an avid yogi) suggested it to me as a way to heal my inner and outer wounds. I brought with me a book I had been meaning to read for some time called *The Heart of the Buddha* by a person named Chögyam Trungpa. I had never heard of Chögyam Trungpa. I wasn't sure what the difference was between Hinduism and Buddhism, or even if there was one. I had never meditated or found myself drawn to Eastern thought, I just liked the title. The Buddha had a heart? I suppose I thought the book was about how the Buddha felt, and if I could get a line on that, perhaps I could learn something about how to handle my own heart. Too, though I read widely in the realms of philosophy, psychology, and sociology, most of the material seemed to lack, well, *heart*. After being nearly killed, I suppose I wanted something softer.

One day I was sitting alone in the retreat center dining hall between meals, reading. The book was fascinating: esoteric and clear at the same time. At some point, I happened on a section that said (and I paraphrase), "The only possible spiritual path is your personal experience." Upon reading this seemingly simple statement, I felt as though my past, present, and future selves suddenly met. A powerful light was illuminated and I saw very clearly how true this was. No doctrine, belief system, or ritual could stand in for personal experience. Even if profound, it would only be so if I could experience the profundity myself and make a personal connection to it. Independence of mind was prized above all. I realized that all of my instincts had always, always directed me according to this belief. In a flash, I saw that this was at the root of my childhood truculence. I was not a bad girl after all. I was fighting to discover, create, and own my experience rather than have it handed to me. *I must be a Buddhist*, I thought. I didn't know that's what it was called.

I finished reading this book and went back to my life feeling quite heartened, but without much further thought about Buddhism or Chögyam Trungpa. I kept that book close by, though, and when I felt scared or doubtful, I would glance at the title. Each time I saw *The Heart of the Buddha*, a feeling of well-being returned.

Fast forward a few years. My guitar-player boyfriend had broken my heart so severely that I could hardly function. (See chapter 8.) In a frenzy, I read countless philosophical, spiritual, and self-help books. Finally, I just couldn't take it and moved out of Texas to take a job at a record label in Boston. (By this time, the Austin nightclub had started a record label that I worked at and thus had embarked on a career in the music business.) I had lived in Boston briefly before and thought, well, anything is better than this funk. I have to break the spell. I have got to get *out*.

Move, new job, crying, reading, working, reading, crying: these were basically my life, especially reading. (And crying.) Some books were complete bullshit. Others were quite powerful and began to change the way I thought. Then I noticed something funny. Each book I read that was particularly brilliant and transformative seemed to come with the same bookmark tucked inside.

After like the twentieth time of noticing this bookmark, I stopped to read what was printed on it. In addition to listing other books that I had loved, it said "Shambhala Publications." Hmm, I thought, one company has produced all of these amazing books. I wonder who those people are and where they are. They must be in some far-off and beautiful place where people are sane and soulful and live according to a different code. Perhaps deep in the Himalayas or atop a skyscraper in Manhattan or some other place far beyond the ordinary world I inhabited. I turned the bookmark over. "Boston," it said. Boston. They were in my town. Shambhala was *right here*. (And remained so until 2015.)

I knew I had to scam a way to meet them. (Which was how I thought in those days.) So I made something up. I called Shambhala and said that I was the VP of sales and marketing for a record label (which was true) and had they ever thought of distributing their audiobooks to music stores? (Which was a silly idea.) For whatever reason, their VP of marketing agreed to meet me. I showed up (at *Shambhala!!*) with my cockamamie idea and a lot of longing. Longing to find out where I belonged. Longing to meet people who knew things I needed to know. Longing to feel at home somewhere, anywhere. I wheeled my Trojan horse of an idea in the door and all I knew was that once they let me in, I was going to find some way to stay.

What actually happened was that we went out to lunch and drank martinis. Their then-VP of sales, Dan, was a great guy who was fun to talk with. Once we dispensed of the ostensible reason for our meeting, we realized we enjoyed talking about marketing and selling, contrasting our industries, comparing notes. Occasionally I would sneak in a question about a particular author or book but then we'd quickly return to talking shop. And drinking martinis at lunch.

One day, we were in another crowded noisy restaurant and I said, you know, I think I might like to learn meditation.

I have no idea what made me say that. I didn't know it was true until I said it but the moment I did, I knew it was and the atmosphere shifted radically. It was as if all the ambient noise and hubbub dropped away. His eyes locked onto mine. "What kind," he asked. I paused. There were different kinds? I heard myself answer, "Tibetan?" "Oh," he said, "I know someone who might teach you."

A few days later, Dan called to say that this person did not have time to teach me meditation but if any other possibilities occurred to him, he would be back in touch. In the meantime, would I come to a party to celebrate Shambhala's anniversary? Wait, what? Partying with the Shambhalians? Yes, I would be there.

At the party, he introduced me to the person who was too busy to teach me meditation. "I hear you want to learn to meditate," he said. "I'm leaving town for a month, but if you're still interested give me a call when I'm back and I'll teach you."

Long story short: I marked the days off on my calendar and called the day after he returned. He did indeed teach me to meditate and not just how to meditate, but the point of view behind meditation as a path to wisdom and kindness. It turns out that he had been an extremely close student of Chögyam Trungpa, the Tibetan meditation master and author *The Heart of the Buddha*. Chögyam Trungpa had taught *him* how to meditate and now he was going to teach me. I felt so lucky.

This turned out to be true beyond imagining. (He is still my meditation instructor.)

I've been a meditation practitioner ever since, and in 1995, I took vows to formally became a Buddhist. I have never looked back.

APPENDIX A

• • •

FAQs

When I first started teaching meditation via the Open Heart Project, I simply sent out videos of meditation instruction. Each week, I would send out a new one. Eventually, people started emailing me with their questions, everything from "What should I do if my foot falls asleep?" to "When I try to meditate, I remember all the things I'm sad about and can't stop crying—what to do?" So I began answering one of these questions before each meditation, and that is how the current video format of the Open Heart Project evolved into a short "dharma talk" followed by meditation.

As new people signed up, I started hearing many of the same questions over again. The questions below are truly the most frequently asked. Then, shortly before sending this manuscript off, I polled people on my Facebook page for their personal questions. The list below reflects both the questions I hear from my own students and those cheerfully offered by my Facebook community. With thanks to both!

Why should I meditate?

Meditation introduces you to the way your mind really works so that it supports your intentions and aspirations instead of thwarting them. Meditation also gives your mental processes a rest, so that when you need them, they're strong and fresh.

How often should I meditate?

Eventually, it's best to try to meditate a little bit every day. Frequency is much more important than duration. Ten minutes a day every day is preferable to an hour every Sunday. If you don't have ten minutes, try to take a few moments on the bus on the way to work or before falling asleep to tune in to your breath and let your mind relax. If you're stuck in traffic, it's not a good idea to meditate, but you can turn off the radio, shut off your cell phone, slow down, and let yourself enjoy the quiet.

Is meditation hard to learn?

Meditation is not hard to learn. It takes about fifteen minutes to learn the technique. It's actually a return to your natural mind state, not the acquisition of a new one, so you already know how to meditate, you just may not know that you know.

What happens if I skip a day?
It's okay. Skipping a day (or a week or a month) is something to pay attention to but feeling bad about doing so is absurd and unnecessary, not to mention destructive. Don't make yourself feel so guilty that you never want to practice again. Just return to it the next day. And remember: feeling bad is optional.

Do I have to sit on the floor?
If you can sit comfortably on a cushion on the floor, great. If not, it's perfectly fine to sit in a chair. You will get the same benefits. Just be sure to follow the same posture instructions.

I'm busy from morning till night. How can I possibly make time for this practice?
To begin, just meditate for five minutes at a time. That is totally great. Then, when or if you feel so inclined, try to fit in two five-minute sessions per day. If even this is too much, you could meditate for as little as one minute—at your desk, on the bus, or anyplace you can sit quietly. You could even connect with the mind of meditation for a few seconds by turning your attention within and simply allowing it to rest on your breath.

All that said, once you begin, I promise you will find that fitting in five, ten, or even twenty minutes per day of meditation is not only doable, it is delightful. You can do it!

I worry that Buddhist meditation practice may interfere with my commitment to the Christian [or other] faith. I don't want to be made to feel that I'm going to have to choose. As my practice deepens, will I?

No. You will never have to choose. It is entirely possible to be a lifelong meditator and a lifelong Christian (or Jew, Muslim, atheist, and so on). Buddhism is a nontheistic religion. In fact, it might better be called a philosophy. There is no God to believe in or outside power to worship, so there should be no conflict.

My teacher, Sakyong Mipham, has said that a mind that is tamed will serve us on any journey we wish to undertake. In this sense, a meditation practice is likely to be wholly compatible with your religious affiliation because it isn't attempting to supplant any part of your spiritual life. I mean, just because you're married, you don't have to give up all friendships with other people. You could have as many friends as you like. Good friends do not interfere in your primary relationship and can serve as a fantastic support when you need some perspective. In just this way, a connection to meditation can support your spiritual inquiry along any lines.

That said, we may run into difficulties if we move from practice to practice or create a hodgepodge by choosing aspects of different practices and blending them. When it comes to traditional practices that are thousands of years old, we can trust that all the details are there for a reason and the benefits of meditation practice come when we go deep rather than broad. So, sure, do whatever practices you like. But don't mix them together.

However, if you decide at some point that you want to actually become a Buddhist, then it is important to make a clear commitment to the path. Committing to a path is akin to getting married, which you only do when you find someone with whom you'd like to share your life. Obviously this option only works if you're head over heels in love.

Meditation can be very boring. Am I stuck? Doing something wrong?

Actually, you're probably doing something right. You are slowing down. Resistance to the form is dissolving. Your mind is settling. Normally, your mind is on a zillion things at once: problems, opportunities, conversations, responsibilities, promises, disappointments, television shows, advertisements, dreams, errands, exercise, transportation, scheduling—and this is just an average day. During meditation, you ask your mind to let go of all of that and instead focus on one thing: your breath. Rather than having unending occupations, suddenly there is only one. It's like giving a kid a doll to play with when she is used to computer games. She'd be like, *What am I supposed to do with this? It doesn't do anything. I'm bored.* Well, yes. Things just got really simple and although at first it is agitating, at some point, you settle down. Besides, isn't it kind of interesting to see how boring most of your thoughts are?! There's not really a whole lot going on in the discursive theater of your mind. The good stuff lies just beyond.

Meditation master Chögyam Trungpa Rinpoche has said that boredom is actually a sign that things are beginning to go really well.

How do I know if I'm doing it right?
If you're applying the technique and able to remember to return your attention to the breath, there is almost no way you can do it wrong. However, there is also no way you can do it right because conventional views of right and wrong just don't apply.

The poet Rumi said, "Out beyond ideas of wrong-doing and right-doing, there is a field. I'll meet you there." This practice takes place in that field.

People report all kinds of amazing experiences and insights while meditating, but I never experience any such thing. Maybe I'm just not spiritual enough. Am I missing something?
No. Everyone's experience of meditation is different. By the way, the instruction for relating to amazing experiences during practice is the same as the instruction for relating to thoughts: gently let go and return to the breath. In fact, "amazing experiences" are considered

distractions. If they happen, it's not a big deal. If they don't, it's also not a big deal. The point of the practice is to experience your actual life rather than to levitate or get rushes of energy. It is better for amazing stuff to happen in your life rather than during your practice.

Personally, I am with you on this. I have never had any earth-shattering flashes, shocks of energy, or found myself suddenly transported into another way of seeing reality. Oh well. However, when I look back on my life since beginning to practice, I see that tremendous transformation has occurred. It must have happened (and still happens) in funny little sideways motions or in some dimension that I simply cannot grasp with my conventional mind.

What am I trying to accomplish by meditating? There has to be a point to it all—I've got a lot of things to do and I can't waste time on something that isn't going somewhere. Let the answer to this important question be revealed rather than predetermined. Meditating with a goal or in order to accomplish something is not giving the practice a fair shake. Instead, let yourself off the hook for having to be productive every moment of the day. Step off the self-improvement treadmill and simply be with yourself in your natural state. The practice isn't about achieving something. It's about letting go. Then, instead of constantly trying to crank something up, *get something to happen*, something starts happening to you.

Meditation is really interesting in this way. It is a creative act, and just like when you sit down to write or compose or paint having preplanned every single step, you end up with a lifeless piece of work. However, if you sit down with a loose idea of where you're headed and then allow yourself to create by feel rather than having a game plan, you end up with something that is at least interesting. The force moves you rather than the other way around, and your innate wisdom, divine consciousness, big mind, smartest self (whatever you want to call it) has a chance to assert itself. So, this is a practice where the point is revealed rather than predetermined. Just get in the car and see where it goes. It's an adventure.

What if my leg falls asleep or I have an itch? Can I move?
Yes, but move mindfully. When you notice the urge to move, wait a moment. Notice what it all feels like: the sensation and then the urge to relieve the sensation. Take its measure and notice the qualities of, say, "leg asleep" (tingly, hot-cold, pulsing, for example) and "urge to change" (perhaps there is a pressing sensation or even a mild shortness of breath) instead of responding to it automatically. Then, once you have noticed the particulars, shift to noticing what it feels like to move your leg so that blood flow is reestablished. Then resettle into your meditation posture and reestablish attention on breath.

I'm really loving this and want to share it with everyone in my family. Can I teach them how to meditate?

Definitely tell them about it! But for them to learn it, it's preferable to direct them to a meditation center for instruction from an experienced teacher. (See Appendix C: Resources.)

People only have one chance to receive meditation instruction for the first time, and although it is fairly simple to explain how to do it (sit down, notice breath, come back if distracted), it is best for them to be introduced to the practice by one experienced at doing so. As mentioned in chapter 7, teaching meditation is as much a transmission as it is an explanation.

Should I try to get other people to meditate?

Only if they bring it up first. Imagine how you would have felt if someone told you to meditate before you came to the conclusion yourself—it might have been off-putting. If you want those you love (or simply have to be around, whether you want to or not!) to meditate because it would be good for them (or, let's face it, make it easier for you to be around them . . .), the most convincing argument is not what you say, it is how you are. The ideal circumstance is one where they ask you why you seem calmer or look fresh or seem to have suddenly developed a hilarious sense of humor (hallmarks of the meditator). Then, tell them!

Will I not be able to function or get things done if I meditate every day?

Meditation does not put you into a stupor—in fact, it sharpens your mind and your senses and generally enables you to function better.

If you dwell on the here and now, how do you plan or think about the future?

Maybe it is unnecessary to point this out, but it is not possible to dwell on the here and now. Once you dwell, here and now are both gone. In meditation there is a sense of nondwelling more than anything else, actually. That said, I don't think that is the spirit of this question. The assumption is that if you are continually bringing your attention into the present, you risk being carried away by the tides of change rather than intelligently crafting the life you want. Also tucked into this question, perhaps, is the idea that meditators are attempting to achieve a state of blandness and nonreactivity, as if the "here and now" were a place where you don't feel or do anything. But of course we have to think about the future and make intelligent financial, emotional, and professional plans. Planning for the future is not an abnegation of the meditative state, nor is goal-setting, strategizing, or owning your hopes and dreams and all the longing that goes along with them. When you sit down to plan, you can be totally aware of *that*. When you think about your goals, be totally aware of *that*.

When you research strategies, be totally aware of *that*. How do you feel in your body? What mental processes are at work and where does your chain of thought lead? Does it make you happy, nervous, sad, confused, all of the above? Rather than not thinking about the future, notice what it is like to be you, thinking about the future. There is no conflict. Awareness is something you bring to wherever you are and whatever you feel more than it is a way of strong-arming yourself into a preferred state of mind.

I've tried to meditate before, but I can't clear my mind of thought. Is it possible that some people simply can't meditate?

There is no need whatsoever to clear the mind of thought, stop thinking, or think only peaceful thoughts. The idea in meditation is to rest with your mind as it is, including those times when it may be speedy, sleepy, agitated, blissed-out, grumpy, dull, or all of the above.

I like the shamatha practice that you teach, but I also like what I've learned from Zen and shamanic healers. I can blend it all to create my own personal practice, right?

In almost all cases, this is really not a good idea. That said, maybe you are the next Buddha and have discovered the spiritual practice that will benefit all of humankind. However, barring that, while it is awesome to explore as many spiritual paths as you like, it is not awesome to explore them at the same time by jerry-rigging a personal system. Seriously. Don't do that. If you want to practice shamatha, practice shamatha. If, the next day, you want to practice zazen, practice zazen, and if the day after that, you want to go on a shamanic healing journey, by all means, go on that journey. Just don't cherry-pick aspects of each practice and blend them together. For example, you may really love sitting zazen *and* contemplating your animal spirit guide. Each is a truly wonderful practice. But if you catch yourself thinking, "Maybe instead of using my breath as the focus of my attention in zazen, it would be cool to focus on jaguar (or bear or wolf or eagle) and in this way harness the power of each practice," hoist the red flag. These are profound and powerful practices and each deserves to be approached with respect and according to its own directives. So take on as many practices as you like, but do them sequentially not concurrently.

And bear in mind that, just like dating, it can be really fun—and informative, important, clarifying— to play the field. Someday, you may fall in love and decide to devote yourself where the most love can be found. Then the whole situation deepens. Though you can't force such things, when they come along, they mark important a crossroads, so pay attention.

I fall asleep during meditation and it is so frustrating. What is going on?

This is one of the questions I hear most often. It is caused by a serious condition we must each be wary of. *It is called fatigue, people.* We are all just so freaking tired. The reason for this is . . . wait for it . . . we are really busy and aren't getting enough rest. (Super insightful of me, I know.)

When we sit down to meditate, we relax. When we relax, we feel what we have been straining not to feel. For many, many of us, that is exhaustion. So, we doze off. There are two next responses to consider. First, it may simply be best to take a little nap rather than meditate. Don't be so hard on yourself. Second, you could simply be with your fatigue as you practice. Where does it live in your body? How does it impact your heart? What does it do to your thoughts? And so on.

Finally, a little tip: when your mind feels too loose as you practice (tired, unfocused, spaced out) you could experiment with putting a *little* more emphasis on the in-breath. It rouses a sense of strength to do so. Similarly, when your mind feels too tight (speedy, frightened, anxious), experiment with slightly more emphasis on the out-breath. This can be calming. Then, when you feel more balanced, come back to the normal practice of equal attention on in- and out-breaths.

How do you know when and if to switch meditation styles?
If you started with concentration, how do you know when
to switch to a more open style? Do people stay with one
style their entire lives? What are the pros and cons for stay-
ing or switching?

There is no better analogy, once again, than romantic
relationships. Imagine if this was the question: "How
do you know when and if to switch partners? If you
started with Bob, how do you know when to switch to
Biff? Do people stay with one person their entire lives?
What are the pros and cons for staying or switching?"

The answer is, nobody knows the answer. You are
the final arbiter. Just as with relationships, you could
learn from past experience, talk to your friends, and
consult experts. But in the end, the only person who
can make these decisions is you. That said, as mentioned previously, switching meditation styles has a
lot in common with switching lovers, and choosing a
particular style has much in common with deciding to
commit versus remaining a free agent. There are pros
and cons in all choices. However, if you want to know
who you are, how much you can give, and are willing
to venture into uncharted territories in the name of
love, commitment is the only way.

I've been taking instruction from your Open Heart Project
for a long time . . . But it's only one day per week. How
do I guide my own meditations or meditate without the

instructions? How or when should I give up reliance on this guidance to sit on my own?

There is only one way to figure out how to do this on your own and that is to . . . do it on your own! Just try it.

Once you have heard the guided meditation enough times, experiment with sitting on your own. You already know how to practice: Take the posture, place attention on breath, allow thoughts to be as they are, and, should you become absorbed in them, let go and return attention to breath. If it would be useful, just remind yourself of these simple steps as you sit down to practice. To track time, use a kitchen timer, an alarm clock, or meditation timer app downloaded to your mobile device. Set it for five minutes. See how it goes. When you feel more confident, set it for ten minutes, or however long you like.

Come back to a guided practice when or if you feel that you need a reminder, or whenever you want.

Another way to experiment is to start out with the guided practice but then, once the instruction is over, turn it off. Set your own timer for five or ten or twenty minutes and see what happens.

In all cases, remember: you can totally trust yourself. So give it a try.

Why should I meditate seated on a cushion? Can't I just stay mindful while doing the dishes, watching football, or driving around town?

If you can stay mindful while doing the dishes and so on, that is fantastic and highly recommended! However, the seated practice is what teaches us how to be mindful in the first place. Part of its power is that it helps you to be more naturally mindful in all situations. But to replace seated meditation with football or dishwashing is kind of putting the horse before the cart, if you know what I mean.

I just can't meditate sitting down. I am too antsy. My meditation is running (or swimming or yoga or dancing). That is okay, right?

Yes, it's okay! But it is not meditation. Meditation, in my book (and, hey, this is my book!!), refers to a specific and time-honored technique for cultivating awareness as well as concentration, compassion, wisdom, authenticity, and so on. Running (or swimming or yoga or dancing) may happen to have benefits (even profound ones) that extend beyond the physical. However, I would not call these things meditation. I would call them "meditative." Anything that marries mind and body or synchronizes breath and movement (as do each of these activities) brings us into a state of relaxed absorption. That is awesome. But meditation and meditative are not the same. So, if you want to run, etc., and feel great about the full mind-body benefits of such activity, by all means, you should. But if you want to meditate, meditate.

How do I create a peer-led sangha (in the middle of nowhere)?

(*Sangha* is the Sanskrit word for spiritual community.) It is really not easy to figure out how to find sangha when there is none! I can suggest a few options, however none of them are quick or easy.

First, you could join an online community. I created the Open Heart Project Sangha (a paid subscription program within the Open Heart Project) for exactly this reason—there are many more people who don't live near a dharma center than those who do. I am making a concerted effort to provide the instruction, guidance, classes, and communal gatherings that a physical center would. I realize this is not the same as being with actual humans! But at least it is something and, actually, it is surprisingly intimate and warm.

Second, sometimes there is only one choice: become a dharma teacher yourself! Instead of going somewhere for the dharma, become the place that people go to. I know this can't be easy where you are, but if you can travel a little or take online programs, you may find a way to become trained as a meditation teacher. Then you could start your own informal gathering and meet periodically to read a book together or simply have a discussion. Build what you are looking for, in other words. I'm not saying this isn't a *huge* commitment on your part because I know it is. Still, it is an option.

Finally, please see www.susanpiver.com/shn
-resources for a guide I've created to starting a meditation sitting group at home.

*Must you be alone to meditate in the midst of everyday
life?*
While being alone in a quiet house is ideal, it is not required. If you live with others, all you need from them
is a promise not to talk to you or step on you or basically interrupt you in any way. They can talk to each
other, do the dishes, even watch TV—and you can
still meditate. It's not as easy, of course, but complete
quiet and isolation are rare. It is far more pragmatic to
cultivate a practice in the midst of daily life rather than
apart from it.

Some years ago, my brother lived in Shanghai. He
was telling me about the incessant *noise* and crowding
and utter lack of privacy wherever you went, even in
your own room. I asked him how he could possibly
meditate under such circumstances. He said, "Well,
if you can practice in Shanghai, you can practice anywhere." Truth. He then lived for a time in Washington,
D.C., which to him seemed like a spacious paradise of
quietude. It's all relative.

*How can I meditate when I am extremely worried about
something and can't take my mind off of that?*
This is an excellent question. When we sit down to

meditate with a lot of anxiety or obsessive thinking, meditation can make it *worse*—if in meditation, we try to shut it down rather than feel it. Sometimes we simply can't let go of our thoughts. If, after some time of attempting to do so, you conclude that it is simply not possible, no problem. You can still meditate. Make one important switch: instead of making your breath the object of your meditation, make your anxiety its object. (I recognize this does not sound fun—it isn't.) Take your attention off of your breath and place it instead on your anxiety. Now, please listen to the next refinement to this instruction because it is of the utmost importance: place it on the feeling of the anxiety *not the story* behind it. In other words, notice how it feels to be anxious. Do you hold anxiety in your belly? Chest? Shoulders? Does it feel hot or cold, sticky or slippery? Does it pulse or is it constant? This is what I mean by feeling. Usually, our attention promptly jumps from the feeling to the story behind the feeling: *I wouldn't feel this unless . . . It is all my fault because . . . I am doomed and there is no exit . . . If this happens, then that will happen, and then I will lose . . .* If you notice that your attention has become absorbed in the narrative, let it go, just as you would let go of thoughts in meditation practice. Return your attention to the felt-sense of anxiety. Then, when you are able, let go of anxiety as the object of your practice and resume attention on breath.

If you are unable to do so, it is no problem. Try again tomorrow. Be gentle with yourself.

What if I have a really good idea during meditation? Can I write it down?

I love this question because I have tried my damnedest to sneak around it. Being a writer and all, this is a real temptation. My art! My art! Not even meditation is more important. *Not.*

So, I have two answers to this question. One is the correct answer. The other is what I myself do.

Correct answer (*do this!!*): Notice your idea, let it go, and return attention to breath. Trust that it will still be there when your meditation session ends. (It will be, say, 90 percent of the time.) No writing during meditation.

What I do (*don't do this!!*): Sometimes, especially when I am in the midst of a big writing project, an idea for what or how to say something grabs hold of me and won't let go. It is so frustrating and plus, I really, really do not want to lose it. If I keep trying to ignore it, my meditation practice consists of, well, ignoring it.

Once, during a thirty-day meditation retreat, I had some fantastic idea (god knows what it was) and *knew* it was the answer to all my problems. But no way was I going to jump up and write it down. In desperation, I looked down at my left thumb and said to it (I had been sitting for quite a while, people), *I'm putting my idea in you and you damn well better hold on to it for me.* Then I forgot about the idea. Until I had another one—which I placed in my right thumb. And another one, which went in my left knee. And on and on. Fortunately, the meditation session ended before I had the chance to *riddle* myself with my own notions. However, the kicker: When I looked at my left thumb, that idea came right back to me. When I looked at my right thumb, the idea I had deposited there also came back to me. And so on. *Don't do this.*

How can I push past the resistance that keeps me from meditating every day? Whether it's fear, busyness, putting it last on the list, it's always the thing that gets cut. I'm sure this has to do with some level of resistance on my part.

This is the maha-question of questions. Thank you so much for asking it.

How do good habits take root? Actual scientists are working round the clock to answer this question. There is a developing body of knowledge about how time of day, companionship, accountability, reminders, and community are needed to support real change. I agree. All of these are great. So, definitely, try to practice at the same time each day. Get a meditation buddy, someone who will also practice in their own home for, say, ten minutes a day at the same time as you. Sign up for newsletters that offer regular reminders about how good spiritual practice is. Try to sit with others from time to time. For example, if you lived in Boston, I would suggest dropping by the Boston Shambhala Center on Sundays to sit with a group. There is something really good about practicing alone and practicing with others.

Okay, all of that is fine. Now I want to comment on the resistance piece of your question. The way you phrase it makes me think that you are walking around feeling bad about yourself for succumbing to the mysterious "resistance." If only you were stronger! Braver! More certain! Well, sure. I would like to be those things too. And, hell, maybe you do have a wicked case of resistance, in which case, please get to the bottom of it. However, I posit that the resistance itself is not the problem. Beating yourself up for having resistance is. Lack of self-compassion is, in my experience, the primary obstacle to meditation practice.

So, sure, try hard and don't stop trying to get to the cushion. But when you run into difficulties (and we all do), choose a different practice on the spot. Rather than sitting meditation, do the practice of being gentle toward yourself. This is a surprisingly difficult, profound, and extremely advanced practice. I am not even kidding.

The practice of meditation is the practice of gentleness. But you don't need to sit on your cushion to do it.

The more gentleness you can extend toward yourself, interestingly, the more fierce and committed you will become. Your difficult emotions are much more likely to respond to your friendship rather than your fear.

APPENDIX B

• • •

important figures

Below are selected names in chronological order of past and current seminal figures in the Buddhadharma. To create an exhaustive list would require many volumes. Those mentioned herein are both important to me and connected to the traditions discussed in this book.

Check my website at www.susanpiver.com/shn -resources for links to learn more about these extraordinary people. If anything catches your imagination, pursue that interest! Find out more about this person and what they teach. I promise, you will thank me.

In chronological order:

Historical Teachers

GAUTAMA BUDDHA
Circa 563 B.C.E. to 483 B.C.E. (different scholars have varying opinions on exact dates)

ASANGA AND VASUBANDHU
Fourth century C.E.
Major exponents of Abhidharma, or "Buddhist
    psychology"

BODHIDHARMA
Fifth or sixth century C.E.
Traditionally credited as the patriarch of Ch'an or
    Zen

NAGARJUNA
Circa 150–250 C.E.
Founder of the Madhyamaka school of Mahayana
    Buddhism

PRAHEVAJRA (Tib.: Garab Dorje)
Circa 55 C.E.
First recorded teacher of Dzogchen or "The Great
    Perfection"

PADMASAMBHAVA
Eighth century C.E.
Called the "Second Buddha" by Tibetan Buddhists;
    responsible for bringing the dharma to Tibet

SHANTIDEVA
Eighth century C.E.
Author of the influential *The Way of the Bodhisattva*

YESHE TSOGYAL
Eighth century C.E.
Main student and consort of Padmasambhava;
   meditation master; considered a female Buddha

TILOPA
988–1069
Taught Mahamudra; considered a seminal figure in
   the Kagyu school of Tibetan Buddhism

MACHIG LABDRÖN
1055–1149
Powerful female Tibetan Buddhist meditation master
   who developed the practice of Chöd, a means of
   tapping into the power of dark energies

DÜSUM KHYENPA
1110–1193
The first Karmapa of the Kagyu lineage of Tibetan
   Buddhism

HONEN
1133–1212
Founder of the Pure Land school of Mahayana Buddhism

DOGEN ZENJI
1200–1253
Founder of the Soto school of Zen Buddhism

NICHIREN

1222–1282

Founder of Nichiren Buddhism

TSONGKHAPA

1357–1419

Founder of the Geluk school of Tibetan Buddhism
 (the lineage of the Dalai Lamas)

HAKUIN EKAKU

1686–1768

Influential teacher of Rinzai Zen Buddhism

MIPHAM THE GREAT

1846–1912

One of the most legendary scholars and masters in
 the Nyingma tradition of Tibetan Buddhism

Modern Masters

SHUNRYU SUZUKI

1904–1971

Seminal figure in bringing Soto Zen teachings to the
 West; author of *Zen Mind, Beginner's Mind*

DILGO KHYENTSE RINPOCHE

1910–1991

One of the towering dharma masters of our age;
 Vajrayana wisdom holder and teacher

TULKU URGYEN
1920–1996
Powerful, kind Dzogchen and Mahamudra master

S. N. GOENKA
1924–2013
Most renowned vipassana teacher of our age

CHÖGYAM TRUNGPA
1939–1987
Tibetan meditation master; brought the Shambhala
    Buddhist teachings to the West

Current Teachers

THICH NHAT HANH
b. 1926
One of the most respected Zen masters of our time;
    founder of Plum Village, a monastery and retreat
    center in France

HIS HOLINESS THE FOURTEENTH DALAI LAMA
b. 1935
Head of the Geluk school of Tibetan Buddhism and
    leader of the Tibetan government-in-exile

PEMA CHÖDRÖN
b. 1936
Prolific author and senior Shambhala teacher who

is gifted in translating the dharma for Western students

BERNIE GLASSMAN
b. 1939
Leading Western Zen teacher and founder of Zen Peacemakers

TULKU THONDUP
b. 1939
Brilliant, prolific, compassionate Buddhist scholar and meditation master

JOSEPH GOLDSTEIN
b. 1944
Vipassana teacher, scholar; cofounder of the Insight Meditation Society

JACK KORNFIELD
b. 1945
Author, vipassana teacher, and deeply respected voice in American Buddhism; cofounder of the Insight Meditation Society

CHOKYI NYIMA
b. 1951
Teacher, scholar, Kagyu master

SHARON SALZBERG

b. 1952

Vipassana teacher known for her insights and
teachings on the practice of lovingkindness;
cofounder of the Insight Meditation Society.

GINA SHARPE

b. ?

Founder and guiding teacher of the New York Insight
Meditation Center

TARA BRACH

b. 1953

Leading Western vipassana teacher and clinical
psychologist

DZONGSAR KHYENTSE

b. 1961

Contemporary Nyingma master and filmmaker

SAKYONG MIPHAM

b. 1962

Shambhala lineage holder and brilliant teacher

BRAD WARNER

b. 1964

American Soto Zen priest and punk rock musician

DZIGAR KONGTRUL
b. 1964
Contemporary Nyingma master

TSOKNYI RINPOCHE
b. 1966
Contemporary Kagyu master

NOAH LEVINE
b. 1971
American Buddhist teacher and author of *Dharma
Punx*

YONGEY MINGYUR RINPOCHE
b. 1975
Contemporary Kagyu master

THE SEVENTEENTH KARMAPA, OGYEN TRINLEY
DORJE
b. 1985
Lineage holder of the Kagyu school of Tibetan
Buddhism

DILGO KHYENTSE YANGSI RINPOCHE
b. 1993
The reincarnation of Dilgo Khyentse Rinpoche

APPENDIX C

• • •

resources

Further Reading

Turning the Mind Into an Ally by Sakyong Mipham
I am not recommending this book because Sakyong Mipham is my teacher and I love him. I am recommending it because it is one of the best books ever written about Buddhist meditation. It is so direct. It is so warm. It is so clear. I have read it many times and it never ceases to shower me with insight.

Cutting Through Spiritual Materialism by Chögyam Trungpa
Early in my practice, I asked my meditation instructor what I should read to gain additional insight into the practice. Without hesitation, he recommended this book (and *Zen Mind, Beginner's Mind* by Shunryu

Suzuki, see below). Now, as a meditation instructor myself, I make the same suggestions. This book is a primer for making your practice a route to liberation rather than to additional confusion.

Shambhala: The Sacred Path of the Warrior by Chögyam Trungpa
There is nothing I can say about this book that would praise it adequately. It may be the most important book of my life. It is a guide to living your life as a fearless, tender, brilliant, kind warrior.

Zen Mind, Beginner's Mind by Shunryu Suzuki Roshi
This book also stands as one of the best books ever written about the practice of meditation. Although I don't practice zazen, I find that every word also applies to my own practice because Suzuki Roshi cuts through cultural forms to reveal the heart essence of meditation practice. How does one begin a meditation practice? What is the correct posture? What is the point of meditation altogether? This book answers these questions in a way that is both bracing and expansive. Thank you, Suzuki Roshi.

On Becoming an Alchemist by Catherine MacCoun
Yes, a book on alchemy—because, for me, it provided a long-missing link between my personal practice and the wisdom energies I have longed to connect to.

Written by an actual alchemist with a deep history with and connection to meditation practice.

Also Recommended

The Way of the Bodhisattva by Shantideva
What the Buddha Taught by Walpola Rahula
The Three Pillars of Zen by Philip Kapleau Roshi
The Art of Happiness by His Holiness the Dalai Lama
Mindfulness: A Practical Guide to Awakening by Joseph Goldstein
Start Where You Are by Pema Chödrön
Radical Acceptance by Tara Brach

For In-Person Meditation Guidance

Shambhala centers: www.shambhala.org/centers
Vipassana teachers: www.dharma.org/teachers
San Francisco Zen Center (affiliated groups): http://sfzc.org/zc/maps.asp?catid=1,11
Zen centers (nationwide): http://sweepingzen.com/category/zen-centers
American Zen teachers: www.americanzenteachers.org/practice.cfm

Work with Susan

If you would like to work with me, I would be delighted. There are several ways you may do so.

Subscribe to the free Open Heart Project newsletter to receive a weekly meditation instructional video from me (and the occasional announcement and special offer; your email address will never be shared). Here is the link to sign up: www.susanpiver.com/open-heart-project/newsletter.

Become a member of the Open Heart Project Sangha to work more closely with me and receive weekly meditation instructional videos, a monthly video dharma talk, free admission to my online classes, and participation in a monthly check-in. Visit this link for details: www.susanpiver.com/open-heart-project.

Sign up for Start Here Now, an eight-part self-paced program to help you explore the themes in this book while establishing a strong meditation practice: www.susanpiver.com/shn-resources.

ACKNOWLEDGMENTS

The following people supplied great questions to include in the FAQ section: Leann Harris, Jennifer Matesa, Donna Morris, Tom Pearson, Marjatta Molmas, Alfred Smith, Paula J. Kelly, Shari Hunt, Mike Gray, Celie Correa, Heather Seggel, Travis Newbill, and Diane Castaldini.

It truly takes a village to write a book, and for me that "village" is my amazing online community, the Open Heart Project. Every day, thousands of people all over the world sit down to meditate together, and their commitment, curiosity, and independent thinking inspire me in ways I can never sufficiently repay them for. Seth Godin appeared out of the blue one day to offer encouragement and friendship. His generosity and wisdom astound me. Thank you for being a soul brother.

My wisdom dakini sisters, Emily Bower, Crystal Gandrud, Eden Steinberg, Stephanie Tade, and Kate Lila Wheeler, are especially appreciated for their brilliance, generosity, and insight into the dharma. What incredible friends you are.

Stephanie Tade, in addition to being a friend, is a deeply supportive agent and I am grateful for our karmic bond. I thank my editor, Beth Frankl, for her encouragement and support, and for simply loving this book. That means the world to me. Thank you to Ben Gleason for a careful and helpful review of this manuscript.

My husband and partner, Duncan Browne, is truly my rock. Thank you for loving me.

Finally, I want to acknowledge and thank the powerful force for basic goodness that is Shambhala Publications. It is an honor to be published by you. Respect, respect, respect.

ABOUT THE AUTHOR

Susan Piver is the *New York Times* best-selling author of eight books and founder of the Open Heart Project, an international mindfulness community that provides ongoing meditation instruction and support.

The Open Heart Project is the best way to stay in touch with Susan. To learn more, visit www.susan piver.com

By the confidence of the golden sun of the Great East,
May the lotus garden of the Rigden's wisdom bloom.
May the dark ignorance of sentient beings be dispelled.
May all beings enjoy profound, brilliant glory.